Praise for Kim Chalmers

My friend and sister in Christ, Kim Chalmers, has written a book that fills a great need among women in the church today, *Supporting Sisters: A Biblical Approach to Helping One Another Through Life's Struggles.* Her study on compassion alone is worth the book, but you will benefit from it all! It is our obligation to edify, admonish, and comfort one another as Christian women. Her book will help us do that ... and do a better job of it. Thank you, Kim!

— Debbie Kea, Rex, Georgia.

Kim Chalmers, with her experience and expertise, has brought a book that is needed now more than ever. As ladies, we face a challenge to support and uplift as never before. Kim provides practical, credible, and biblical advice on topics ranging from empathy to effective communication. This book is an excellent grounding tool for Christian women in today's ever-changing world.

— Cayron Mann, LPC, Florence, Alabama.

This book could be a game-changer in your own life and help leave a legacy of faith-filled comfort in the lives of your sisters. All of us walk through valleys on our way to heaven. All of us come to points at which we need someone to listen—to truly care about our circumstances and give sound advice rooted in the Word. Kim has done a superb job of presenting biblical and practical truth for women who are willing to be active listeners for sisters who are struggling. She, through this book, will give you confidence. She will make you know that you can help women navigate the dark days that are sure to come in every life. She gives us a resource that prepares regular, ordinary women in Christ to become extraordinary comforters and helpers to other women in the family of God. I am sure that I will personally refer back to the simple, but effective strategies presented in this well-researched work. It is a work that will strengthen the sisterhood.

— Cindy Colley, Huntsville, Alabama

Supporting Sisters

*A Biblical Approach to Helping One Another
Through Life's Struggles*

Kim Chalmers

CYPRESS

Copyright © 2025 by Kim Chalmers

Cataloging-in-Publication Data

Chalmers, Kim

Supporting sisters: a Biblical approach to helping one another through life's struggles / Kim Chalmers.

p. cm.

ISBN: 979-8-89733-001-0 (pbk.); 979-8-897-33-002-7 (ebook)

1. Women—Christian life. 2. Women—Religious aspects—Christianity I. Author. II. Title.

248.86—dc20

Cover design by Brad McKinnon and Brittany Vander Maas.

For information:

Cypress Publications
3625 Helton Drive
PO Box HCU
Florence, AL 35630

www.hcu.edu

As I was in the process of writing this book, I reflected on sisters in Christ that I have known throughout the years. Sisters whom I leaned on when I was struggling, sisters who said an encouraging word to me at just the right time, sisters who walked alongside me as we raised our families, and sisters who prayed with me. No matter where you live, you will find sisters in the Lord's church who will encourage you, love you, and offer support in times of joy and sadness. This unique bond of love and friendship as sisters binds us together through our Father. For all sisters in Christ, I dedicate this book to you.

I pray this book will help you support sisters who are struggling and who need encouragement while drawing one another closer to Christ. We always want to reflect God's love in everything we do, and supporting sisters allows us to do just that!

Contents

Supporting Sisters

Foreword

A depressed and anxious friend has asked you to meet her for lunch. Another woman (who has been visiting your Tuesday morning ladies' Bible class) shared with you that she is going through a divorce. Your neighbor's husband recently passed away. You would like to help each of these women, but you don't feel equipped to help. You fear saying or doing the wrong thing. You tell yourself to leave counseling to the professionals, but there is still a nagging feeling that you need to do more than take a casserole to a bereaved family. Your anxious friend needed more than a Chicken Salad Chick pick 2 combo, and an unchurched visitor going through a divorce needs more than your pity. Kim Chalmers's book, *Supporting Sisters: A Biblical Approach to Helping One Another Through Life's Struggles,* is an outstanding resource to assist you in becoming the helper you would like to be.

While I was teaching graduate counseling classes at Heritage Christian University, Kim Chalmers enrolled in the University to begin work on her Master's in Ministerial Counseling. In talking with her, I learned she wanted to help Christian women through the struggles of life. She wanted to equip herself to help and to help other women support and encourage others. Chalmers's love for the Lord and His church is evident in her speaking and writing. Her heart is filled with love for her spiritual sisters and a desire to strengthen the church by equipping women to support one another.

As a Licensed Professional Counselor, I have always been on the lookout for useful tools to help my clients—and to help my clients learn to begin to help themselves. Chalmers's book is definitely one of those useful tools. The book is filled with best practices from the field of counseling. The skills of active listening, confidentiality, empathy, and others discussed in the book are widely accepted as the ingredients of effective helping and ethical practice. Chalmers explains these skills in a way that would benefit helpers at all levels of skill or education. Her discussions of these skills within the book include biblical examples as well as practical application. Chalmers wisely includes a chapter on "How to Know When to Refer." An important part of being an effective helper is recognizing that you are not always the best person to help an individual. Sometimes, making a referral to someone may be the best way to help.

The greatest benefit of the book for the Christian woman looking to learn how to help others is the biblical foundation that underlies everything discussed. As Chalmers states in the book, God and His Word are the foundation, and Christ is the cornerstone for all the Christian does, including counseling and supporting fellow Christians. Chalmers's ability to link biblical teaching and examples from Scripture with the application of counseling and support is enlightening and encouraging as a Christian uses the information from the book to help and counsel fellow Christians. Chalmers identifies examples from the Old Testament and the New Testament with both men and women in the role of helper. We can certainly learn from these examples. Chalmers wraps up the book with a chapter discussing the most important ingredient in effective helping: prayer.

In reading this book and applying its principles, you will be better prepared to be a helper regardless of your level of expertise in counseling. If you apply these principles in your life, you will, in fact, be more Christ-like in all your relationships with others.

Rosemary Snodgrass
Florence, Alabama

PART 1: Laying the Foundation

(Why Women Should Support Each Other and Preparing Yourself to Support Sisters)

Introduction: Christ as Cornerstone

Most women like to talk. I believe I can make that statement because I do. We like to share our feelings, joys, struggles, and heartaches with each other. Many women have a circle of friends whom they feel they can discuss the most intimate details of their lives. This is good and needed because women have different struggles, perspectives, and motives, and they experience emotions differently than men. Because of this, women encounter various stages of good mental health throughout their lives. The woman who has just had a baby, who has suffered a miscarriage, who is trying to juggle her responsibilities working outside of the home along with her family obligations, who is the caregiver to others, who has just sent her last child off to college, who is experiencing middle age, or who is entering her twilight years, is experiencing emotions, thoughts, and concerns that a man is not in a position to relate. Women need women to lean on, learn from, and be encouraged by. But, sometimes it is hard to know how to react and respond to a sister who needs to share personal information and how to best support her, even though the Bible directs us to do just that.

I became keenly aware of the importance of knowing the right thing to say to those struggling during the early days of the COVID-19 pandemic of 2020. Some of my friends and family members wanted to discuss their fears, concerns and struggles they had during this time. I also struggled with the same fears, concerns, and struggles and felt I was ill-equipped how to respond. Like most women, I want to "fix" problems. However, in this unique period we as a society found ourselves experiencing, I was unable to help. A short time later, I knew I wanted to be educated on how to help people who were struggling, so I completed a master's program in Ministerial Counseling. The knowledge I gained has given me the confidence to counsel sisters in Christ. From studying Scripture, it became apparent to me that, as Christians, we should be willing and able to support those who are struggling.

In Galatians 6:2, we are to "bear one another's burdens and so fulfill the law of Christ (ESV)." This verse is directed to the body of Christ as a whole (women included), not just elders or ministers. As Christians, we have a responsibility to care for each other, not only in times of physical illness but in spiritual illness as well. In order to effectively support, counsel, and care for others, Christians must be equipped. Ephesians 4:12 states to "equip the saints for the work of ministry, for building up the body of Christ." Equipping the saints comes in the form of education and training. Education and training will allow women to serve as supporters to our sisters who are struggling. A researcher interviewed three women who engage in a Women's Counseling Ministry, and they discussed the importance for women to be trained to support and help other women who are struggling. All three women concurred, "It's also important to remember that the majority of people who seek out counseling are women, so the need for women's voices in the care of women in the church is really important."[1] They also discussed the reality that counseling happens in informal settings, so the need to equip the saints is vital. This leads to a thought-provoking point: "Whenever people speak into each other's lives, counseling is taking place. Since this is true, it raises the question: Is the counseling that is happening in the church coming from well-equipped followers of Jesus?"[2]

While many Christian women have wise counsel that would support others, some feel they are inadequate and ill-equipped to offer such counsel. I recently surveyed seventy-eight women who are members of the Church of Christ, ages 17–85. Sixty-eight percent of the women stated they did not feel equipped or qualified to counsel other sisters. [3] As Christian women, we are often called upon to counsel our sisters. This book is written for all Christian women, particularly those who seek better ways to support one another in times of need. While this book also assumes you have had no training in the field of counseling, if you do have formal training, the book will reinforce the principles of Galatians 6:2, Ephesians 4:12, and Titus 2.

As we begin learning how to better equip ourselves to support sisters, I would like for us to equate that process to building a house. If you have ever been involved in the process of building a house, you know that there is an order of construction that must occur. For example, you cannot put a roof on without having the foundation laid first. There is also a process for supporting sisters. Certain elements must be in place in order to effectively support sisters. We will begin by focusing first on establishing a foundation with Christ as our cornerstone. A cornerstone is the first stone set in the construction of a masonry foundation. All other stones will be set in reference to this stone, thus determining the position of the entire structure.

Isaiah 28:16 states, "Therefore thus says the Lord God, Behold, I am the one who has laid as a foundation in Zion, a stone, a tested stone, a precious cornerstone, of a sure foundation: 'Whoever believes will not be in haste.'" This Scripture is referring to Jesus Christ. Christ is our cornerstone of everything we do. Without Him, nothing in life really matters. The Bible clearly teaches how Christians should support and help one another. A house will not be supported without a cornerstone, just as we cannot support others and be supported by others without Christ.

In the chapters that follow, we will discuss the importance of building the right kind of foundation that is needed to support sisters. The Bible will serve as this foundation. We will notice the pattern of biblical counseling we see in God's word and discuss why it is important for women to support other women who are struggling. We will learn the importance of preparing our hearts and minds so we can be effective in supporting sisters. We will then discuss basic counseling tools such as how to actively listen, how to improve communication, how to demonstrate compassion, how to demonstrate empathy and the importance of prayer in the supporting process. All of these tools are scripturally based and will give us insight as to how they were used in Jesus's ministry. Finally, practical tips will be given so you can learn and apply them when supporting our sisters in Christ who are struggling.

Because I am not a licensed professional counselor, I understand my limitations and would never presume I could counsel on that level. So, we will discuss the importance of knowing when to refer someone to a professional counselor and the benefits that would entail. Woven throughout the book, we will see a pattern of these tools used by the Master Builder, Jesus (Hebrews 4:3–6).

Women, in general, feel more comfortable talking to

another woman than to a minister or elder regarding certain issues. Because of this, women who counsel women are more helpful because they understand the emotional, physical, and psychological makeup of women. In any counseling or conversation you have with someone, the first step is to "do no harm." Simply stated, this book will provide you with the tools to incorporate basic counseling principles to help and support sisters in your life who might be struggling.

It is my sincere prayer that this book will bless you and enable you to offer support, encouragement, and love to sisters in Christ who are in need!

Chapter 1

Biblical Support of Counseling

Where there is no guidance, a people falls, but in an abundance of counselors there is safety.

— Proverbs 11:14

The Bible as the Foundation: Part 1

ANY STRUCTURE that is built must have a foundation. When a child begins playing with his or her Legos or blocks, they always make sure they have a flat, sturdy surface to start. They know if they start out on an uneven, soft surface, whatever they are building will come crashing down.

We are familiar with the parable recorded in Matthew 7:24–27 about a wise man building a house upon a rock instead of the sand. We know without a doubt a firm foundation keeps a structure stable and secure.

The Word of God serves as the foundation upon which the Christian life is built. The foundation we have in the Word is what permeates all decisions we make in life. Without the foundation of the Word, our spiritual lives will crumble. This most often leads to sin problems and the inability to live a life in obedience to God. Everything we encounter in life and the reactions we display, whether from good or bad experiences, must have the Bible as the foundation. When things are going well in your life, we praise God for His blessings and give glory to Him. When things are not so well, we also praise Him for His blessings and give glory to Him while looking to His Word for comfort. For Christians to live a life that is stable, secure, and abundant, God's Word must be our foundation (Philippians 4:19, Isaiah 33:6).

When we are supporting sisters, our personal foundation must be firm and unwavering. We are to be bold and courageous while being loving and supportive. Being bold and courageous means as supporters, we always look to God's Word for answers (2 Timothy 3:15–17). In this chapter, we will look at the foundation of biblical counseling we find in Scripture. In Chapter 2, we will continue the theme of foundation and notice a pattern we see regarding women-to-women counseling.

Counseling Observed in Scripture

When you hear the word counseling, you might think of an office where a person is lying on the couch and a doctor is taking notes on what the person is saying. This is the stereotypical image that comes to mind. However, counseling can take place in other venues with different groups of people. According to Merriam-Webster, the word "counsel" means advice given, especially as a result of consultation.[1] On a daily basis, counseling takes place informally at kitchen tables, in the church parking lot after services, over a meal, or any place where, at a moment in time, people need support from one another. Counseling may take the form of an older mother supporting a new mother who is struggling with getting a newborn to sleep. Counseling may take the form of a woman who has been married for a number of years listening to a young newlywed who is having a tough time adjusting to married life. Counseling may take place between two mothers who are experiencing an "empty nest" for the first time. There are many scenarios where women support other women in their everyday lives. Many times, those who need support will seek wise counsel from fellow Christians, but some may choose to seek counsel from those with a worldly perspective. In order to support others, we must know what Scripture says about how we should counsel others and then become equipped to be helpers. As Christians, we should always seek guidance from Scripture to help us navigate life's struggles and, in turn, support others.

As we study Scripture, we see support for counseling sprinkled throughout the Bible. If you are like me, it takes several readings of a passage to begin to understand the truths a passage holds. But, as we read the Bible with a "counseling lens," we will begin to see the rich truths the Bible holds regarding the support of counseling. In the Old Testament, a counselor usually refers to "those who give counsel."[2] This type of counsel is referred to as advice, or consultation given in connection with political and military leaders (see 2 Samuel 15:12 and 1 Chronicles 27:32–33) and comforter or helper (see John 14:16, 14:26, 15:26, 16:7; 1 John 2:1). Notice a few examples of counseling we see in Scripture:

- King Rehoboam sought counsel from old men (1 Kings 12:6).
- Saul sought counsel about finding his father's lost donkeys (1 Samuel 9)

- David sought counsel from Ahithophel (2 Samuel 15:12)
- King Artaxerxes had seven counselors. (Ezra 7:14, 28)
- Nebuchadnezzar surrounded himself with counselors (Daniel 3:24–27, 4:36, 6:7)
- Apollos was counseled by Priscilla and Aquila (Acts 18:24–26)
- Jethro counsels Moses (Exodus 18:19)
- Solomon wrote about the importance of counselors. (Proverbs 11:14, 12:20, 15:22, 24:6)

What Is Biblical Counseling?

Before we are able to support others in the way God intended, we must understand what biblical counseling involves. Biblical counseling may be defined as a type of counseling that is pursued when people who are struggling with life's problems need support from someone who is empathic and compassionate and shows Christian love to others. That "someone" in the previous sentence refers to Christians. The very essence of who a Christian is involves helping, serving, supporting, and loving others. Galatians 6:1 asserts those who are spiritual (or mature Christians) should help to restore those who are in sin. 1 Peter 2:9 refers to Christians as a royal priesthood, and as such, we are to be Christlike and support our sisters. Those who seek biblical counseling need guidance to understand and to know the kind of life Jesus wants them to live.

Counseling involves change. A change usually takes place in one's behavior, mindset, and/or environment. One essential element regarding biblical counseling is that Jesus Christ does not change (Hebrews 13:8). The love and care that Jesus has for us is constant. In Romans 8:31–39, Paul declares that no matter how difficult a situation might be, Christians cannot be separated from the love of Christ. As we offer support to our sisters, we want to remind them of God's unwavering love and hope He has for His children. God wants us all to repent of sin (Mark 1:15), be faithful to Him (Revelation 2:10), and lead a productive Christian life in service to Him and others (Hebrews 6:10). The message of love and hope is important to convey to those who are struggling. Let us consider the greatest example of biblical counseling we have (Jesus) and also note some occasions where Paul demonstrated support to others.

Jesus, the Best Example

Jesus is the best example of how to counsel biblically. Throughout Scripture, we see a pattern of Jesus asking the right questions to people to gain information, listening attentively to others, showing empathy and compassion to all, and communicating effectively. Later in this book, we will focus on specific counseling skills that Jesus demonstrated to those He came in contact with, but first, I would like for us to consider the way Jesus interacted with the Samaritan woman at the well and the conversation He had with Martha when He came for a visit.

The account of the Samaritan woman at the well is recorded in John 4. This Samaritan woman came to draw her water from the well during the hottest part of the day; other women would have come in the cool hours of the morning. The first question when reading this account is, why did the Samaritan woman draw water during the hottest part of the day? Had she been treated unfairly by the other women? Was she ashamed of her lifestyle, and it was just easier for her to go to the well when others were not there? Scripture does not give us an answer. We can only infer her reasons.

Jesus came into contact with her and held a conversation

that would change her life! We know that this encounter was unique as Jews did not have contact with Samaritans. But Jesus, who knew the answers to the questions before He asked, met her where she was—physically and spiritually. He knew her home life and knew she was in sin. People who are engaged in sin are not, by definition, in a good place spiritually but perhaps not even emotionally or physically.

They are not in the presence of God. God and sin cannot coexist. People who need support may or may not have sin involved, but they do need someone to be present, like Jesus was with the woman at the well. Notice people who are on the outside looking in; you may be the example they need to help them through their struggles.

Jesus first asked something of her, "Give me a drink." He did not criticize her about her lifestyle or even acknowledge who He was. She could fulfill his immediate need to "give me a drink." People want to feel needed. This will help develop trust in a relationship that will allow the person to open up to you. She had the ability to fulfill His request. Nobody wants to feel like a "project." Of course, some people are so broken they are not ready to serve or help. However, you can walk alongside them when they are. When and if they come to the point where they can feel needed, this will increase their confidence and give them hope and purpose. Maybe it is as simple as having them come with you to visit someone. Find out what they are comfortable with and give them an opportunity to help.

Jesus gave her the opportunity to tell Him what she wanted Him to know. He already knew about her background. But, because we cannot know every facet of someone's story, we rely on them trusting us enough to talk. Let them tell us what they want us to know. We may be mistaken about what we think we know and be surprised to learn things differently. Jesus does not dwell on her past, and He does not tell her everything that she did was wrong. He focused on the future and on hope. Always find common ground with someone. Focus on shared experiences and on similarities of likes and dislikes. This will build trust, and only then can you begin to teach them about the love of Christ. We will discuss how to build trust in a later chapter, but the example of Jesus and the woman at the well is an excellent example for us all.

Another example of biblical counseling involves the account of Jesus's visit to Mary and Martha's house in Luke 10. Martha was busy preparing a meal for Jesus while Mary sat at Jesus's feet listening to His teaching. Martha was frustrated that Mary was not helping her. So much so that she asked Jesus to tell Mary to come help her! Jesus knew the best way to respond to her. He expressed deep concern for her by starting His conversation with "Martha, Martha."

He knew she was anxious; He even tells her so in Luke 10:4. By His response, Jesus lets Martha know, "I see you and I hear you." He did not rail against her about how wrong she was. He did not tell her to "calm down" or ask her, "Why are you getting so upset? Don't act that way!" He let her know there was a better way, at that moment in time, to respond to the situation. He acknowledged that what she was feeling was important, but He wanted her to remember the priorities or "the good portion" and to make sure she felt heard and understood.

The tone and words we use when helping others can either make a situation better or worse. Jesus, in His infinite wisdom, knew the right words to use to let Martha know He cared for her. By His tone and His words, Martha then realized what Mary was doing at that moment in time was far more important than being concerned about meal preparations. We will discuss the importance of verbal communication when supporting sisters in a later chapter.

Paul as Counselor

The Apostle Paul also provides a good example of how to support others. We see through Paul's epistles his common theme was the teaching of the death, burial, and resurrection of Jesus Christ.

Throughout the New Testament, we have a record of Paul's counsel and encouragement given to others. He offers guidance on a broad array of topics such as unity among Christians, sexual immorality, boastfulness, not engaging in activities that would make a brother stumble, behavior before and during marriage, the older teaching the younger, how to resolve conflict, behavior of Christians, worship, and the use of spiritual gifts. Paul, through the Holy Spirit, provides counsel on topics that are just as applicable today as they were during Bible times. Let us note two examples of Paul's specific support and guidance of others and what we can learn from them.

The account regarding Euodia and Syntyche's conflict at Philippi is familiar to us. We are not told what the conflict was, only that there was a conflict, and Paul was concerned the conflict would have a negative impact on the church at Philippi. Paul asks the "true companion" to step in and help the sisters find a resolution to the conflict. We know from Philippians 4:2–3 that Euodia and Syntyche had labored alongside Paul in spreading the gospel. Paul could not be present to support and offer counsel to Euodia and Syntyche as he was in prison during this time.

But he did feel that it was important enough to enlist another person's help with the situation. We do not know exactly who this "true companion" was, but we can conclude that he or she was someone that Paul trusted to conduct this helping. Paul was not in the habit of "calling out" people in his writings, so for him to name Euodia and Syntyche outright, he must have been very concerned. We also are not told how or if the conflict was resolved, but a lesson we can learn from this passage is the fact that Paul saw a need and made provisions to help Euodia and Syntyche to come to a resolution. Oftentimes, we do not want to get involved in situations, especially conflict between sisters in Christ, but as Christians, we must try to help so conflict will not cause disunity within the church. Most people are uneasy when dealing with conflict, but if they have the proper tools at their disposal, it might make unpleasant conversations easier. We can assume the "true companion" had skills that helped Euodia and Syntyche resolve their conflict without damaging the church at Philippi.

In Acts 15, we read the account of Barnabas, John Mark, and Paul. Barnabas wanted John Mark to accompany him and Paul in visiting the brethren. Paul did not think bringing John Mark along was best. Scripture tells us in Acts 15:39, "and there arose a sharp disagreement, so that they separated from each other." So, Barnabas and John Mark went one way while Paul and Silas went another. We are not told of the specific problem between John Mark and Paul, but we do know that they eventually resolved their differences (2 Timothy 4:11).

If Paul and Barnabas had handled this another way, the Lord's work could have suffered. This is a worthwhile example of knowing when to keep silent in a situation. They agreed to disagree, separated, and continued in their ministry. We can assume sin was not the reason for the disagreement, as Paul would have wanted to address that. So, when sin is not involved and there is a question of opinion, tradition, or ego, it is sometimes best to let it go and move on.

When helping others, it is just as important to know when not to speak as it is to know when to speak, as we will see in later chapters.

Big Picture

As Christians, we are to be helpers. We are to serve others, let our lights shine, and offer hope and love to those who are struggling. The Bible gives Christians a pattern to follow when helping and counseling others. We must remember the accounts given in the Bible are those of people who had the very same emotions that we have today. They, too, struggled with sin and the stresses of everyday life, and they needed support. Christ designed the Christian life not to be lived alone but to enjoy fellowship one with another. Christians are to rejoice together in happy times and to weep together during difficult times. As we all strive for our eternal reward, let us remember to love, help, support, and care for one another.

Questions for Discussion

1. Think back to a time when you gave counsel to or received counsel from others. Did this counsel help the situation? Why or why not?
2. Discuss three of the circumstances surrounding the examples of counseling given in the chapter.
3. How did this effective counseling help each situation?
4. If you have been asked to give counsel to a sister in the past, how did you respond? Did you feel confident in your counsel? Why or why not?

Chapter 2

Biblical Support of Women to Women Counseling

Therefore encourage one another and build one another up, just as you are doing.

— 1 Thessalonians 5:11

The Bible as the Foundation: Part 2

As we discussed in Chapter 1 regarding the Bible as the foundation for our support and we identified through Scripture the pattern of counseling others, let us now turn our attention to what the Bible says concerning women counseling women. The question that you might be thinking is, "What's wrong with men counseling women?" The short answer is "nothing," but I believe the better question that should be asked is "Are men always in the best position to counsel women?"

Listening, encouraging, advising, supporting, and offering hope are actions that are sprinkled throughout the Old and New Testaments. Jesus is the perfect example of all these actions. But, because of our imperfections as humans, we do not always provide the appropriate counsel. Let us look at the story of Hannah and see how Eli responded to her.

The story of Hannah is found in 1 Samuel 1 and 2. Hannah had longed for a child of her own for a long time. Her husband Elkanah had another wife, Peninnah, who was able to give Elkanah children. Every year, they traveled to Shiloh, where families offered their sacrifices and worshiped God. Seeing families carrying out this gesture must have been hard for Hannah to witness. Peninnah would provoke Hannah just to irritate her because she could not have children.

This went on for years, and because of Peninnah's behavior toward Hannah, Hannah wept and would not eat. Elkanah did not understand why she was crying and would not eat. 1 Samuel 1:8 reads, "And Elkanah, her husband, said to her, "Hannah, why do you weep? And why do you not eat? And why is your heart sad? Am I not more to you than ten sons?" Poor Elkanah was clueless about how Hannah felt. A woman, on the other hand, would have known exactly why Hannah was feeling the way she was. She was being mistreated by the mean girl (Peninnah), and her heart ached for a child. A woman would have been more insightful and understanding of Hannah's behavior.

Later, Hannah comes into contact with Eli, the priest. She is still distressed and begins praying while she weeps (ESV adds "bitterly"). Her prayer is simple: if you give me a child, I will give him to serve You all the days of his life. Eli sees her praying and assumes she is drunk. She replies to him that she is a woman "troubled in spirit." She also tells Eli that she has been "pouring her soul out to the Lord" and she was "speaking out of great anxiety and vexation."

Again, a woman would not have jumped to the conclusion that Hannah was drunk and would have been able to comfort her. She would have had an intuition as to why Hannah was feeling so distraught, while a man would not. While Eli eventually realized what was wrong with Hannah and was able to comfort her, telling her to "go in peace," a woman would have been able to provide the appropriate support and comfort to Hannah from the beginning.

Women simply have a unique perspective about how other women are feeling. Women have a sense of "kinship" because we all go through similar stresses in life, such as childbearing, midlife, and societal influences about "doing it all," that a man does not encounter. We can lean on our experiences to support each other during challenging times. So, to answer our question, sometimes men are not always in the best position to counsel women.

We also must ask the question, as Christian women, do we have the skills needed to support others? For many, these skills come naturally. But for others, these skills can be learned.

As sisters in Christ, we simply cannot say, "No, I can't help a sister in need." This goes against Scripture; we look to Titus 2 for guidance. In Titus 2:3–5, Paul (through the Holy Spirit) gives women clear instructions on how to best support each other in need. Consider the instructions he gives:

> Older women likewise are to be reverent in behavior, not slanderers or slaves to much wine. They are to teach what is good, and so train the young women to love their husbands and children, to be self-controlled, pure, working at home, kind, and submissive to their own husbands, that the word of God may not be reviled.

In effect, Paul is writing to Titus and calls for same-gender teaching and counseling by the older women to the younger women. Notice that Paul did not instruct Titus to teach the women himself. Hendriksen, in his commentary on Titus, states, "One understands immediately that no one—not even Titus—is better able to train a young woman than an experienced, older woman."[1] Focusing on Titus 2:4, "and so train the young women to love their husbands and children," let us examine the word train. In place of train, some translations use appeal, encourage, urge, advising, sober, meaning serious-minded, self-controlled. The word sober is translated from Greek, which means "to bring someone to their senses." Fitzpatrick and Cornish note that "all these words communicate the idea of coming alongside someone to help him or walk in faithfulness (especially when sinful habit patterns persist in preventing growth)."[2] Receiving wise and godly counsel from an experienced Christian woman would be an encouragement to a younger woman, especially as God has gifted the older woman in this area of ministry. Remember, there is no age listed in this passage. Age is relative to being older and younger. No matter your current age, you are always older than someone who could benefit from wise, godly counsel. Everyone, at every age, needs support in this life. The guidance from the older women to the younger women is needed on how to properly deal with the struggles and stresses of life. However, as we will address later, the methods, tone, and response of the older woman to the younger woman are equally as important as the counsel given.

Paul writes to Timothy in 1 Timothy 5:9–10 concerning the treatment of older widows. The passage discusses the good deeds done by widows as we see in verse ten, "such as bringing up children, showing hospitality, washing the feet of the Lord's people, helping those in trouble and devoting herself to all kinds of good deeds (NIV)." Because Paul is writing to the church in Ephesus to guard against false teachers, these verses suggest that widows engaged in counseling with other women to support those who were weak in the faith.

When older women offer support, encouragement, and wise biblical counsel to the younger women, they are serving God, but they are also showing the love and hope that can only be found through Christ! As we read in 1 Corinthians 3:6–8, we plant the seed, and God will give the increase. God, through His infinite wisdom, has given women a pattern to use to support our sisters. We must use the life experiences and wisdom that God has given to us to help others. I believe many women are hesitant to "get involved" because they may not know the "right thing to say." All we need to do is look at the guidance we find in Titus 2 to make us feel confident in our abilities.

Examples of Women Counseling Women

When looking for specific examples in the Bible of women counseling women, there are few interactions to consider, but we can infer that women-to-women counseling took place in some form. To begin a counseling relationship, trust is needed between two individuals. Once trust has been established, counseling can take the form of serving others, lending a listening ear, supporting those in need, and walking alongside in times of struggle. I believe if we consider the teachings from Titus 2:2–5, Galatians 6:2, and 1 Thessalonians 5:11, the following are good examples for us to examine of women counseling women.

Mary and Elizabeth

We read about Mary and Elizabeth in Luke 1. We know that Mary and Elizabeth were relatives who were also pregnant at the same time. Upon hearing from Gabriel that Elizabeth is with child and that Mary herself would give birth to Jesus,

Mary made the journey to visit Elizabeth. What a happy occasion it was when Mary arrived! "And when Elizabeth heard the greeting of Mary, the baby leaped in her womb" (Luke 1:41). They both realized their pregnancies were indeed gifts from God, and Mary began to sing praises to God. Mary stayed with Elizabeth for about three months, and then she returned home (Luke 1:56). I am sure Mary and Elizabeth had much to discuss during those three months. When I was pregnant with our son, I had a friend who was about three months ahead of me in her pregnancy. We leaned on each other because we were experiencing pregnancy for the first time. Can you imagine the comfort and counsel that Mary and Elizabeth gave to each other during this special time in their lives?

Deborah

The story of Deborah is familiar to us. She was the only woman Judge of Israel, and she was instrumental in guiding the Israelites to victory over the Canaanites. Her story is told in Judges 4.

She would sit under a tree in the hill country of Ephraim, and the "people of Israel came up to her for judgement (Judges 4:5)." As a prophetess, she would speak on behalf of God. She settled disputes between parties and would guide and encourage people to follow God. No doubt, she was a source of counsel to women, given her unique position. God used Deborah to lead the Israelites back to Him. This responsibility was great, and she had faith that God's will would be done.

Dorcas

Dorcas was a woman who lived in Joppa. In Acts 9:36, Dorcas is described as someone who is known for her "good works and acts of mercy." When she passed away, the widows, who were the recipients of the clothes Dorcas made for them, called upon Peter, who was in a nearby town, to come and raise her from the dead. With her prominence among the widows and her service of making clothes for them, we can also assume she was a support and encouragement to the widows. As she interacted with the widows, she must have developed a close relationship with them and was beloved. This is evident from Scripture as we see the outpouring of grief from the community she served. While Scripture does not tell us that she herself was a widow, she felt the need to serve this special group of women. When we serve others, our example and our love for Christ and others speak louder than words. As we see from the reaction from her community upon her death and the fact Peter was urged to help, she was beloved and considered irreplaceable. Given this response, she was empathetic and offered support when the widows needed it the most. Serving others shows a level of love and trust that can aid as support to those who are struggling the greatest.

Naomi and Her Daughter-in-Law, Ruth

The story of Naomi and Ruth reminds us of friendship, faithfulness, courage, and supporting others in times of need. Their story reveals what a strong relationship between mother-in-law and daughter-in-law can look like and what blessings can emerge. Naomi offered advice to Ruth about returning to her homeland because Naomi had no sons alive and had nothing to offer Ruth. Ruth must have loved and respected Naomi because she did not go back to her homeland but stayed with her. I imagine Naomi offered Ruth a listening ear and wise counsel when she needed it. She advised Ruth to stay with the other women in the field so she would be safe (Ruth 2:22). She advised Ruth on how she should attract Boaz (Ruth 3). Ruth had great respect for Naomi to stay with her away from her family and homeland to embark on a new life, not knowing what lay in front of them. They trusted God that He would provide, and He did. When Naomi encouraged Ruth to go back to her homeland (four times), she knew that the decision was Ruth's.

While she offered advice and the advice was not taken, it did not impact their relationship. In fact, Ruth 1:18 tells us that when Naomi realized Ruth was not going back to her homeland, she dropped the subject. When you offer someone counsel and they do not take it, remember it is not a personal reflection on you. Sometimes, people need to figure things out for themselves, often with undesirable consequences, before they are able to make a better choice. Obviously, in the account of Ruth and Naomi, God's providential hand was guiding the decisions of Ruth. But when we are helping others, we must always remind them of God's way and love while offering encouragement and support.

The Virtuous Woman

While Proverbs 31:10–31 gives instructions as to how a Virtuous Woman should conduct herself as a wife, I believe the same instructions can be applied to all Christian women, whether you are married or not. Specifically, I would like for us to consider Proverbs 31:26: "She opens her mouth with wisdom, and the teaching of kindness is on her tongue."

Let us first examine the beginning of verse 26: She opens her mouth with wisdom. While she speaks with wisdom to her household, we can also assume she also speaks with wisdom to other women she encounters. From Scripture, we know her community thinks highly of her husband, and they would know what kind of example she is (Proverbs 31:23). Her community knows of her character by the way she conducts herself in word and deed. Her development of wisdom contributes to her ability to give counsel, and because she is wise, she chooses her words carefully (Proverbs 10:32). She always reflects the love of God to others. She uses the gift of communication that God has given to her to support others. Because of her gentle and quiet spirit, she knows when and how to offer support to others (Proverbs 15:28). When helping others, it is important to know when to stay silent and when to offer advice. She is not speaking just to hear herself, and she is not boasting to everyone about her wisdom. The way we, as Christian women, obtain wisdom is through prayer and staying in the Word (James 1:5, Matthew 4:4, and 2 Timothy 3:16–17). Of all the attributes that are listed in Proverbs 31 about the Virtuous Woman, her ability to offer wise counsel to others cannot be overlooked and should serve as an example for us all.

The last part of verse twenty-six speaks to the teaching of kindness. Simply stated, she is kind with her words and shows love, mercy, and grace to all she speaks with. By her kindness, she is showing the love of God. She also shows women a pattern of how we should behave and how to offer support to others, as shown by her example (Ephesians 4:29). This woman is intelligent and loves God. She is kind first in her heart and then in her speech, demeanor, and deeds. Because of her wisdom and kindness, she is respected, and women will know how they will be treated when they come to her seeking support.

Servant-Minded Women

When we consider 1 Timothy 5:3–16 and Titus 2:3–5, servant-minded women were present in the early church.

Because of the qualifications given in Scripture for men to be elders and deacons, they must be the husband of one wife, we can assume, like today, these women served in ministry and supported their sisters within their churches. In Romans 16:1, Paul describes Phoebe as a "servant." These servant-minded women would have supported their sisters in childbirth, baptisms, sickness, and with the struggles of everyday life. Although we live today in a different time with our modern advances, sisters today are not any different than sisters in Bible times who needed support. Servant-minded women in the early church no doubt supported, counseled, and walked alongside their sisters.

Women at the Cross

The women at the cross all had something in common: they loved Jesus. After witnessing Him hanging on the cross, they had a shared experience, unlike anything they had encountered. There must have been comforting, consoling, and supporting each other as they witnessed the greatest sacrifice known to man! The days after Jesus was crucified could not have been easy, but I imagine they still had to attend to their daily duties. Their grief and pain would have been unbearable in the days after what they had witnessed at the Cross, but to learn three days later that He had risen, what joy they felt. Not only did they share joy, but also the support they must have given each other because of this shared experience.

In conclusion, while Scripture does not tell us every verbal exchange women had with each other, we do see a glimpse about life for women during Bible times. I feel confident that we can conclude that women during Bible times dealt with some of the same emotions and struggles women experience today. From Scripture, we know that women married difficult men (think Abigail), they struggled with infertility (think Sarah and Hannah), they experienced widowhood (think Naomi), they gave birth (many examples), and they experienced the death of a child (think Bathsheba, Rizpah, and Mary). These are just a few examples of struggles that women experienced during Bible times and also experience today. Women need the godly support of other women. They need wise counsel from their sisters in Christ. They need to feel the hope, love, and comfort that only God can give them. One of the greatest examples of being Christ-like is the example of women who desire to support other women during life's most profound struggles.

Questions for Discussion

1. What do you believe are the benefits of women counseling women? Discuss specific examples and scenarios.
2. Today, what are some ways we see the older teaching the younger as described in Titus 2?
3. Discuss ways your congregation fosters or could encourage this type of relationship between the older and younger ladies.
4. How can women-to-women counseling help to create and strengthen healthy congregations?

Chapter 3

Developing the Right Mindset
Identifying and Using the Right Tools

Set your mind on things that are above, not on things that are on earth.

— *Colossians 3:2*

Planning and Reflecting on the House

WE HAVE all observed structures being built in our communities, such as houses, schools, churches, shopping malls, etc. We see different tools that are needed for the construction of these buildings. Everything from heavy machinery such as a backhoe or dump truck, needed to move dirt to hammers and nails. Now, you would not see a hand mixer or a spatula on a construction site because those are not the correct tools to build something. So, in order to support each other, we need to make sure we have the correct tools. Prayerfully, this book will help you to assemble the right kinds of tools to use when supporting sisters. Before we can learn specific tools to help support sisters, we need to examine ourselves from within and take notice of the state of our minds and hearts.

Self-Awareness: Beginning the Process of Planning and Reflection

When you begin the process of building any structure, there is much planning and reflecting involved. You must make sure that what you are building will meet your needs. Learning how to best support sisters also takes careful planning and reflecting. You want to make sure you are aware of your own limits, biases, and abilities so you can be the most effective in supporting sisters. The ability to become self-aware equals the ability to be a healthy supporter for our sisters.

Self-Awareness is having a conscious knowledge of one's own character and feelings. It is a form of self-reflection where we clearly examine our state of being, our feelings, our actions, our behaviors, our strengths, and our weaknesses.[1] 2 Corinthians 13:5 tells us to become self-aware by examining ourselves. "Examine yourselves, to see whether you are in the faith. Test yourselves. Or do you not realize this about yourselves, that Jesus Christ is in you? —unless indeed you fail to meet the test!" Paul is reminding the church in Corinth that self-examination is good, so we might have a faithful life in Christ.

Self-Awareness teaches us to better understand how uniquely God created us. When we are aware of our own feelings, actions, behaviors, strengths, weaknesses, and motives, we will be better equipped in supporting others. We must know who we are as individuals and, more importantly, as Christians before we can support others effectively. In a sense, it is the beginning of our own self-improvement. Reflect on your experiences, see what God has done for you, and how He has helped you through challenging times. This will allow you to be more compassionate and empathetic when supporting sisters.

Scriptures Concerning Self-Awareness

Scripture tells us that it is important to be self-aware. We certainly see times when Paul and Jesus demonstrated self-awareness. Consider the following verses:

- "Keep a close watch on yourself and on the teaching. Persist in this, for by so doing you will save both yourself and your hearers" (1 Timothy 4:16).
- Paul was completely self-aware. "But by the grace of God I am what I am, and his grace toward me was not in vain. On the contrary, I worked harder than any of them, though it was not I, but the grace of God that is with me" (1 Corinthians 15:10).
- Paul examined his current existence and declared, "I am ready" (2 Timothy 4:6).
- Paul examined his history as a Christian and said, "I have fought, I have finished, I have kept the faith" (2 Timothy 4:7).
- Paul examined his future hope and said, "There is a crown for me" (2 Timothy 4:8).
- "The purpose in a man's heart is like deep water, but a man of understanding will draw it out" (Proverbs 20:5).
- "For by the grace given to me I say to everyone among you not to think of himself more highly than

he ought to think, but to think with sober judgment, each according to the measure of faith that God has assigned" (Romans 12:3).

- Jesus knew exactly who He was and His purpose. "Jesus, knowing that the Father had given all things into his hands, and that he had come from God and was going back to God, rose from supper. He laid aside his outer garments, and taking a towel, tied it around his waist. Then he poured water into a basin and began to wash the disciples' feet and to wipe them with the towel that was wrapped around him" (John 13:3–5).

Importance of Self-Awareness When Supporting Sisters

When you are self-aware and have a deep understanding of your own thoughts, emotions, and feelings, this understanding will help you relate to sisters who are struggling in a more meaningful way. Because supporting sisters is personal, it is important for you to be aware of certain thoughts and emotions that a supporting environment might provoke. We are to be Christ-like in all of our thoughts and emotions, and self-awareness will play a vital role in how we serve God and our sisters. Becoming self-aware will also highlight our own biases we may have and if those biases would hinder us in supporting our sisters. Issues regarding sin are non-negotiable. We must call out sin for what it is and help our sisters navigate repentance. However, biases such as choosing at what age to marry, choosing to homeschool, choosing to work outside of the home, or parenting decisions are issues that, if you take a firm stand one way or another, may hinder support for a sister who is struggling. When supporting sisters, you want to be the avenue that God can use to do His will, not yours.

Self-awareness will make you aware of things such as your communication skills, both verbal and nonverbal, and your level of compassion and empathy, which we will discuss in later chapters.

Finally, becoming self-aware will allow us to recognize our own past experiences, help us to understand our sisters better, and Lord willing, support them to the best of our ability. As we become self-aware, we will be able to take what we have learned about ourselves and model to others the importance of their own self-awareness. When a sister who is struggling is able to become self-aware, her awareness will help her to foster healthier relationships and cope more effectively during times of struggle.

In order to effectively support a sister, there are basic characteristics that must be present. This begins with a self-evaluation of your mindset and heart. Having the proper mindset and heart to help someone is important so that the person being supported will feel safe, secure, and loved. A structure cannot be built with incorrect tools, just as the support you offer can not be effective if your mind and heart are not aligned with supporting others.

Preparation of Minds and Hearts

The Bible gives us a clear pattern of how our minds and hearts should be. Let us look at Scripture to prepare our minds and hearts to support sisters.

- "Search me O God and know my heart. Try me and know my anxieties and see if there is any wicked way in me. And lead me in the way everlasting" (Psalm 139:23–24).

- "You have said, 'See my face.' My heart says to you, 'Your face, Lord, do I seek'" (Psalm 27:8).
- "Do not be conformed to this world, but be transformed by the renewal of your mind, that by testing you may discern what is the will of God, what is good and acceptable and perfect" (Romans 12:2).
- "Set your minds on things that are above, not on things that are on earth" (Colossians 3:2).
- "Therefore, preparing your mind for action, and being sober-minded, set your hope fully on the grace that will be brought to you at the revelation of Jesus Christ" (1 Peter 1:13).

These verses remind us to set our minds and hearts on things of heaven, not of this world. When our minds and hearts are aligned with that goal in mind, we will be more effective in supporting sisters.

Now, let us note specific ways that will help us prepare our hearts and minds to support sisters. They are being humble, being sincere, keeping confidence, building trust, and establishing boundaries.

Being Humble

A humble heart and mind serve others. We are to do nothing out of conceit but to view others more significant than ourselves (Philippians 4:2). Humility is the foundation of supporting sisters.

We are all broken. We all have walked through our own valleys and have also experienced the joy of being on the mountaintops. Our experiences will give us knowledge that we, through God's infinite wisdom, can be used to help support sisters who are in need. Jesus shows us humility in action. He ate with sinners, He washed the feet of the apostles, He ministered to those who were in need, and He paid the ultimate sacrifice of the Cross. We are to strive every day to model His example in our lives. Demonstrating humility will be a blessing in supporting sisters.

Being humble and having genuine intentions work together. Reflect upon why you want to support sisters. Do you believe you have a gift of encouragement, wise counsel, and the ability to support sisters? Do you want to uphold the teachings of Titus 2 in reference to the older women teaching the younger women? Remember, you will always be older than someone! We will talk about confidentiality later in this chapter, but the motivation to support sisters cannot be that you "want to be in the know."

Being Sincere

Sincerity when supporting sisters means you have a genuine interest in others and the struggles they encounter. Philippians 2:4, "Let each of you look not only to his own interests, but also to the interests of others." Paul is clear in his instruction that we are to not only have our own interests, but we are to be interested in what others are interested in. As active Christians, we have busy and full lives working in the Kingdom, but we do not want to be so busy that we cannot support our sisters who are in need. This reminds me of an episode of *The Andy Griffith Show*. Goober had recently purchased the gas station. He was so busy tending to his different responsibilities that came with being a new business owner that he forgot to order the gas! He had customers come to him wanting to fill their tanks with gas, and there was none. We do not want to miss opportunities to support others who are right in front of us because we are too busy with other interests.

We see examples from Scripture of the genuine sincerity of others.

- Jonathan was concerned about the welfare of his family, and David promised to take care of them (1 Samuel 20:14–17, 42; 2 Samuel 9).
- Deborah was sincere in her decisions that would best serve the people she was judging.
- Epaphroditus was distressed because the church in Philippi had heard he was ill. He was sincere in his concern for them (Philippians 2:26).
- Paul spoke of Timothy's concern for the Church in Philippi (Philippians 2:20).
- Jethro was concerned about Moses and his trying to do too much (Exodus 18:18).
- Christ made the ultimate sacrifice of putting our interests above His own in suffering on the cross.

Sincerity is being patient with the sister you are supporting. If you are insincere, many will see through that and conclude that you really do not care. This is not what we want to convey to our sisters who need support. It is not Christ-like, nor will it lead to any productive support. In order to support sisters, we will need to make many sacrifices, especially in time, but that sacrificial love and support is what Christ modeled for us.

Keeping Confidences

When sisters need our support, it is because they are struggling in some way. Usually, sisters do not seek counsel from another unless they are at a low point in their lives and feel desperate enough to seek support. The struggles they share tend to be personal in nature, such as internal struggles like anxiety, stress, unhealthy thoughts, or external struggles of relationships that are unhealthy or even toxic. Because of this, it is imperative that confidentiality during support of that sister is kept. You could characterize what they are sharing with you as a secret. Remember, a secret is something not known or seen or not meant to be known or seen by others. The Bible discusses the importance of keeping confidences. Consider these verses:

- "Whoever goes about slandering reveals secrets, but he who is trustworthy in spirit keeps a thing covered" (Proverbs 11:13).
- "Argue your case with your neighbor himself, and do not reveal another's secret" (Proverbs 25:9).
- "Whoever covers an offense seeks love, but he who repeats a matter separates close friends" (Proverbs 17:9).
- "When words are many, transgression is not lacking, but whoever restrains his lips is prudent" (Proverbs 10:19).
- "Whoever goes about slandering reveals secrets; therefore, do not associate with a simple babbler" (Proverbs 20:19).
- "Besides that, they learn to be idlers, going about from house to house, and not only idlers, but also gossips and busybodies, saying what they should not" (1 Timothy 5:13).

When you support sisters who are in need, it is a great responsibility. You do not want to break confidentiality and share the struggles of hurting sisters and risk losing their souls.

They could become so broken and betrayed they leave the Lord's church. Supporting a sister can be a great comfort to those hurting, and prayerfully, they will draw closer to the God of all Comfort.

Many times, when supporting sisters, personal sin is not involved. The sister just needs someone they can confide in and gain wise counsel. But if sin is involved and repentance is required, encourage the sister to do so. If necessary, offer to go with her to the Elders so they may offer guidance. This may be the greatest support you can offer her. There is no circumstance too great that cannot be rectified through repentance and forgiveness.

If the situation arises that the sister you are supporting needs additional support (another trusted sister who could offer insight into the situation, or they have been through the same experience and are willing to support), always secure permission from the sister to confer with someone else. When you confer with someone else, you desire to help the person and bring them closer to Christ and not spread hurtful gossip or to allude to others that you are "in the know."

Building Trust

In any relationship that includes the support of another sister, you must first build trust. You may be supporting sisters with whom you have a personal relationship, or you may be their acquaintance. So, the question is, how do you build trust?

Building trust with someone is a process. Trust must be earned. Remember our discussion in Chapter 1 about the woman at the well? Jesus began a conversation with her and asked her for a drink. She fulfilled His request, and trust began to develop. Consider the following ways to build trust:

- Always Tell the Truth: The Bible tells us to let our yes be yes and our no be no (Matthew 5:37). Your word is your truth. Always speak truth in love, and this will serve to solidify your trustworthiness (Ephesians 4:15). When your words are followed with Christ-like action, trust will be established. Sisters who need support want to know the counsel you give them is truthful and always according to God's Word.
- Be Transparent: Sisters who are seeking support are vulnerable. They may have experienced trauma or are trying to cope with the stresses of this world. They might feel that they are the only ones who are feeling this way. We are all broken, and we all need support. Reassure them of this fact of this life. This will help to build trust in the relationship as they will know they are not alone. When we are transparent with one another, it helps to bear one another's burdens (Galatians 6:2). This allows us to live the Christian life not in isolation but in the security of our sisters.
- Be Consistent: The counsel you give must always be in accordance with God's word. This will give comfort to sisters who are seeking support because they will know you are committed to following God's word. This comfort will allow them to trust the counsel you are giving. Situations change, but the way we respond should not. Because of this, it is important that you are grounded in the Word and if needed, you should not hesitate to seek out additional support to help others.

Establishing Boundaries

God established boundaries. Boundaries denote where one thing ends and something else begins. In creation, God created a heaven and an earth. That is a boundary. In the physical world, we have mountains or bodies of water that create a boundary. In all relationships, a boundary is created when you decide what you are comfortable with and what you are not comfortable.

This could be a boundary within a verbal conversation or a boundary with what you are willing to do for someone else. As Christians, we should be willing to help others, but there are limits. These limits will be different for everyone. But it is important for you to understand what your limits are. When supporting sisters, you will become emotionally involved because you love her soul and are a sister in Christ. But just like any relationship you have, there should be limits or boundaries within the supporting relationship.[2]

Knowing that you will become emotionally involved when supporting sisters allows you to be on guard that the supporting relationship does not evolve to the point that it starts affecting your everyday life. It is important to remember that it is not your job to "fix" anyone. You are providing support from a place that is wise and biblical to help the sister work through her struggles while growing closer to God. This process can be long and intense. As we see from the way Jesus sent His apostles out in pairs in Mark 6, He created a support system for those supporting others. He also told them in Mark 6:11 to move on if people were unreceptive. If sisters are not receptive to your support, that is all right. They may need time to get their mind in the right place to receive godly counsel. And not everyone will heed your support. It is important not to get discouraged. There will be other sisters who need your support. This is where establishing boundaries becomes important. You always want to make sure you are finding a healthy balance between supporting your sisters and your own healthy mental state. Supporting sisters should not be impacting negatively on your self-esteem, spirituality, or family life. One of the most important steps in the support of others is to evaluate if we have prepared our minds and hearts. This chapter has offered specific ways to do just that, but it really begins with prayer and Bible study. Just as planning and reflecting are keys in building any structure, planning and reflecting are equally as important in supporting sisters. When our minds and hearts are aligned with God's will, He will use us to His glory in supporting sisters!

Questions for Discussion

Engage in self-reflection and think about the following. Journal your answers if you would like.

1. Reflect on the talents that God has given you. If you are unsure of your talents, find a Spiritual Gifts survey online. Determine how your talents can be best used to support sisters who are in need.
2. Are there certain situations that would make you feel emotional?
3. Are there people you consistently have conflicts with? Have you determined the reason and sought to resolve that conflict in a godly manner?
4. Do you feel confident regulating your emotions before reacting to a situation?
5. Do you consider other people's perspectives besides your own?

6. In preparing our mind and hearts to support sisters, which of these do you find yourself struggling with and why? Humility, sincerity, keeping confidence and trust, and establishing boundaries.
7. What boundaries have you set personally in your relationships? For example, your family, church, or work relationships.
8. Do you need to reevaluate and reset boundaries in any of these relationships? I recommend the Cloud and Townsend book for help in this area.

PART 2: Beginning to Build

(Learning How to Support Others)

Chapter 4

Tool 1: Demonstrating Compassion

All of us, at some time or other, need help. Whether we're giving or receiving help, each one of us has something valuable to bring to this world. That's one of the things that connects us as neighbors—in our own way, each one of us is a giver and a receiver.

— Mr. Rogers

Preparing the Land

WHILE WE HAVE BEEN DISCUSSING BUILDING a structure in general terms, let us now focus our attention on building a house. Adequate preparation of land is essential and is the first step in building a house. Our house backs up to the foot of a small mountain. When our neighborhood was being developed, lots were sold on the side of that small mountain. After building a few houses, the builder realized those lots would be too difficult to prepare the land enough to even build a house. So, that land has been left in its natural state; that land has been left unprepared.

When supporting sisters, demonstrating compassion is like having land that has been adequately prepared for development. If you are not prepared to demonstrate compassion to others, the support you provide will not be sufficient. Many people struggle with showing compassion to others, but with study and prayer, demonstrating compassion can be developed and applied. Demonstrating compassion toward others is the basis of supporting sisters, and it is essential. Thankfully, we have a clear pattern of demonstrating compassion that we can study from the Bible. We can discover and model how compassion was demonstrated by some of the greatest examples ever known to man!

What Is Compassion?

The word compassion comes from the Latin *compati*, meaning "to suffer with." Compassion is defined as "a feeling of deep sympathy and sorrow for another who is stricken by misfortune, accompanied by a strong desire to alleviate the suffering."[1] You feel the sadness of the suffering of another person, and you want to take action to try and help lessen the suffering. We all may feel sad, mad, frustrated, or (insert any adjective) when someone is suffering, but some of us do not feel compelled to help ease the suffering. As Christians, we should always desire to help ease (if we can) the suffering of others.

We live in a world of sin. As Christians, we know the damage that sin in our own lives can do, but also what sin in the lives of those we love can do. Many times, our suffering is because of others' sins. When we suffer, this is the time when demonstrating compassion is needed the most. Overall, we tend to experience some degree of suffering more times than not. The degree of suffering varies because of circumstances outside of our control, such as health-related issues, grief, and loss. Our own suffering can also vary because of intrinsic issues such as unhealthy thoughts, anxiety, and low self-esteem. I would like to share with you a story of compassion in action, and as a result, young people's lives were profoundly changed for the better.

Compassion in Action

In 1991, Rose and Eliasar Espinoza moved to Brea, California. They noticed the youth in the neighborhood would hang out in the streets with baseball bats. The issue was that they were not interested in playing baseball. Then, there was a drive-by shooting on the street where they lived, and they began to worry about their family's safety. They began a neighborhood watch group, which was not well received by the neighbors. The sentiment was, "Just mind your own business." Rose realized the kids were raising themselves and were bored. She knew the kids needed to feel like they mattered and belonged. So, she turned her garage into a free after-school K-12 tutoring program. She started by offering homework help and lemonade. Sixteen kids showed up on the first day. She enlisted the help of older kids with good grades, who helped her tutor. This was the first such program in the neighborhood. She realized the kids wanted to learn, and their neighborhood began to be transformed. Within two years, academic scores increased, and crime decreased. Over the years, Rose has opened up other tutoring sites where over two hundred children are served at any given time. The program is still in place today and is known as Rosie's Garage.

Remember the definition for compassion: a feeling of deep sympathy and sorrow for another who is stricken by misfortune, accompanied by a strong desire to alleviate the suffering. This is exactly what Rose was showing the students. The students experienced suffering because they did not feel that they belonged and that no one cared for their well-being. Rose alleviated that suffering by breaking generational poverty through education.[2]

Compassion Demonstrated in the Bible

The subject of compassion being discussed in Scripture is plentiful. Consider a sampling of the following verses:

- "In overflowing anger for a moment, I hid my face from you but with everlasting love I will have compassion on you, says the Lord, your Redeemer" (Isaiah 54:8).
- "As a father shows compassion to his children, so the Lord shows compassion to those who fear him" (Psalm 103:13).
- "When he saw the crowds, he had compassion for them, because they were harassed and helpless, like sheep without a shepherd" (Matthew 9:36).
- "And he arose and came to his father. But while he was still a long way off, his father saw him and felt compassion, and ran and embraced and kissed him" (Luke 15:20).
- "For he says to Moses, 'I will have mercy on whom I have mercy, and I will have compassion on whom I have compassion'" (Romans 9:15).
- "For you had compassion on those in prison, and you joyfully accepted the plundering of your property, since you knew that you yourselves had a

better possession and an abiding one" (Hebrews
10:34).

These verses offer comfort and support to those who are
suffering and in pain. In Scripture, we also see a pattern of
compassion being demonstrated to others. Consider the
following examples:

- Boaz (Ruth 2:15): Boaz demonstrates compassion
  to Ruth as he instructed the workers in his field to
  leave grain for her to pick up. This provided Ruth
  with the food she needed to survive. This is an
  example of compassion and sharing acts of
  kindness with the needy.
- The Widow of Zarephath (1 Kings 17: 8–16): In 1
  Kings, we learn the story of Elijah and an unnamed
  widow. Even though the widow was in great need
  herself, she prepared a meal for Elijah. As an act of
  compassion, God provided the additional oil and
  flour, and she and her son ate for many days after.
- Joseph (Genesis 42): After being sold into slavery
  and then rising to power in Egypt, Joseph showed
  compassion to his brothers when they came to
  Egypt looking for food.
- The Good Samaritan (Luke 10:25–37): The Good
  Samaritan tended to the man who had been robbed
  and beaten and made sure he had a place to rest.
  The Good Samaritan saw a need and acted to
  alleviate the man's suffering.

These are just a few examples of acts of compassion
demonstrated in Scripture. Now, let us study further the
compassion of Christ.

Compassion of Christ

Compassion embodies the concept of the deep mercy of God, the Father. Our greatest example of compassion in the Bible is our Heavenly Father. As Psalm 86:15 reads, "But thou, O Lord, art a God full of compassion and gracious, longsuffering and plenteous in mercy and truth (KJV)."

God's compassion is infinite and eternal. "It is of the Lord's mercies that we are not consumed because his compassions fail not. They are new every morning: great is thy faithfulness" (Lamentations 3:22–23). God comforts His people with compassion.

Jesus exemplified compassion during His ministry on earth. One of the most poignant examples of compassion in the Bible is when Jesus showed compassion at the grave of Lazarus.

When Jesus saw Lazarus's friends weeping, he wept alongside them (John 11:33–35). Over and over, our Lord Jesus Christ felt compassion on people, healing them and comforting them. As with all things good, kind, pure, and worthy, our greatest example to study is Jesus.

At the most unimaginable time in Jesus's earthly life, He still showed compassion to others as He hung on the Cross. Consider the following examples of how He demonstrated compassion to others as He was suffering.

- To the Women: Jesus showed compassion to the "daughters of Jerusalem" who followed Him to the cross. He warned them the destruction of Jerusalem was imminent. Through this warning, He demonstrated concern and compassion for them instead of focusing on what He was about to experience (Luke 23:28–31).

- To the Crowd: Jesus asked God to forgive those who crucified him. When we forgive others, it is a demonstration of compassion (Luke 23:34).
- To the Thief: Jesus demonstrates compassion to the thief in the middle of His own suffering. He showed the thief grace and hope for the next life in Paradise (Luke 23:39–43).
- To His Mother: Jesus, while still on the cross, made provisions for His mother, because "for not even his brothers believed in Him (John 7:5)." He gave the responsibility to John to look after Mary (John 19:26–27). This is a demonstration of compassion because Jesus knew that John would help comfort her after His death.

Now that we have established a clear pattern in the Bible of demonstrating compassion to others, let us discuss specifically how to demonstrate compassion to sisters who need support.

Why Is Demonstrating Compassion Important When Supporting Sisters?

Everyone needs compassion to be shown to them at some point in their lives. When sisters are struggling, they need to feel compassion to help them navigate through challenging times. When compassion is demonstrated, it allows the sister to feel attended to and allows them to see the love of Christ in action.

Demonstrating compassion to sisters who are struggling allows connections and relationships to be established. When we become aware of our sisters' struggles, we can minister to them and also determine better ways to respond to help alleviate their suffering. When we demonstrate compassion to others, we see a firsthand view of how sin affects lives. And that spurs us into action. "Compassion is not an automatic response to another's plight; it is a response that occurs only when the situation is perceived as serious, unjust, and relatable."[3]

How to Demonstrate Compassion to Sisters Who Need Support

The first step in demonstrating compassion to sisters is to become aware of those who are in pain and suffering. Many times, we will greet our sisters with "Are you ok?" Often, the response is "Yes." Sisters who need support will not always be the first to reach out and let it be known they are in need. It is important that we, as sisters in Christ, build relationships of friendship and trust so those sisters who need support will feel comfortable asking for support. The better question might be, "Are you ok, right now?" While we do not want to pry, we do want to make sure our sisters feel supported if they need it. The best way to simply become helpers of our sisters is to notice if they seem "off," under abnormal stress, or are missing services. Let them know they are supported, particularly if they have had a major life event such as the death of a loved one, newly married, have a new baby, or have had a change or loss of a job. These circumstances can often be the most stressful time of a woman's life. When you see someone who is not having an easy time, take the initiative to let them know that you want to listen to them only with the intent of understanding them. After you learn of their pain, then seek to determine if there is anything you can do to alleviate their suffering.

Practical Ways to Demonstrate Compassion

- Choose Your Words Wisely: When a sister is experiencing challenges in her life, be careful with the words that you speak to her and the tone that you use. The adage "less is more" is most applicable when supporting a sister in need. We will discuss the importance of communication in a later chapter.

- Understand Her Point of View: When a sister is suffering and in pain, it is important for her to feel heard. In the moment of pain and suffering, the sister may say things and behave in a way that is irrational. This is a normal response. Be sure that you do not offer judgment in the midst of her pain and suffering. When emotions are at bay, always speak truth in love to that sister. (Zechariah 8:16, Ephesians 4:15)

- Validate Her Feelings: When you validate the suffering sister's feelings, you demonstrate to them that what they are saying or how they are feeling matters. When you listen and accept that she feels a certain way, you make her feel heard, understood, and valued as an individual.

- Simply Ask: "What do you need?": Give the sister time to articulate what she needs at that moment in time. She may need to know that she has the full and unconditional love and support of her church family. She may just need a listening ear, but a chicken casserole dropped off at the front door might also be the comfort and support she needs.

- Respect Her Wishes: Not everyone you offer support to will accept. If someone declines your support, lovingly let her know you are available to support her in any way you can. That might be the most compassionate thing you can do for her at that moment in time. If you find yourself in this situation, do not let it hurt your feelings. This is not the sister's intention; she may not be ready to receive support.
- Offer Hope: When sisters are suffering and in pain, they need to be assured there is hope. Verbalize to them, "It's going to get better." This will be a reminder and an anchor that they can hold on. Words of hope can be a great source of comfort while also letting them know they are loved and supported. (See Isaiah 40:31; Jeremiah 29:11; Micah 7:7; Romans 5:3–4, 15:13.)

Earlier in this chapter, we discussed the importance of preparing land in order to build a house. Just as you cannot build a house without adequately preparing the land, you cannot support others effectively without demonstrating compassion. We all experience suffering and pain. When compassion is shown to us by our sisters, it can be the most comforting feeling we experience. When compassion is shown and received, we see Christ's love abundantly, and what a blessing that is to us! When we demonstrate compassion to a sister, we should not try to know how she feels or what we think is the best way to help. The best way to offer support and extend compassion is to validate her suffering and to listen without judgment, let her know she is not alone, and offer hope for a better tomorrow.

Questions for Discussion

1. Before we demonstrate compassion to our sisters, it is important to be compassionate with ourselves. In what ways or in situations do you demonstrate compassion to yourself?
2. Do you believe that compassion is intrinsic, or can it be learned? Discuss the reasons for your answer.
3. At your congregation, in what way is compassion demonstrated and encouraged?

Chapter 5

Tool 2: Active Listening

Most people do not listen with the intent to understand; they listen with the intent to reply.

— *Stephen Covey*

The Frame

A KEY STEP in building a house is putting up the frame. The frame is erected early in construction so the house will take shape and can move forward in the building process. The frame gives the house structure and helps the builder identify different rooms of the house. Frames also ensure that the weight of a house is distributed evenly. Snow, wind, or people could affect the weight of the house. If the weight is not distributed evenly, the results could be catastrophic. Listening actively also requires equal distribution of attentiveness from the listener's perspective. For us to support sisters effectively, it is important to listen to all aspects of a sister's concerns. Active listening, therefore, is the "frame" around determining the next steps in supporting others and requires you, as the one offering support, to be alert and present in the moment. The tool of active listening is the first step in hearing a sister's concerns, which will "frame" the situation at hand. Active listening will give our conversation structure, which will enable you to discern how best to support sisters. Active listening is a learned skill. When you demonstrate active listening, you are conveying to the sister that she has your full attention and will do your best in supporting her.

What Is Active Listening?

If you have taken college classes or continuing education classes, you might have had instructions on how to speak publicly or how to write a research paper. However, many classes are not offered on how to actively listen. Learning to actively listen is a skill needed in all relationships we have.

Think of how many times you have wondered, "Are they listening to me?" This can occur with work colleagues, church members, family members, or anyone we come into contact with on a daily basis. It can be frustrating! This quote sums up the importance of active listening:

> Listening may be the most important part of communication. It is through listening that we validate each other. It is through listening that we create the opportunity to truly know each other.[1]

If we do not listen appropriately to our sisters, we will not be able to give them the support they need.

Active listening is the practice of preparing to listen, observing what verbal and nonverbal messages are being sent, and then providing appropriate feedback for the sake of showing attentiveness to the message being presented.[2] The skill of active listening is basic when supporting sisters. This skill can be learned and mastered, but also must be practiced. It leads to the beginning of understanding the needs of a struggling sister and will enable you to offer support for the issue at hand.

When individuals are engaged in conversation, parties usually work together. The nature of active listening—making eye contact, limiting distractions, listening for understanding—will create a foundation of understanding. This idea of communication and understanding will be helpful when seeking to assist others during times of struggle. Active listening serves both you and the sister seeking support. From your perspective, it enables you to gain a deeper understanding of the sister and her needs. As you practice the skill of active listening, you will gain an advantage in supporting sisters. When you are able to listen and understand the sister, it is a win-win for all involved. Active listening is Galatians 6:2 in action.

Active Listening in the Bible

Scripture has numerous verses that teach us the importance of listening to others. Simply stated, we listen to others because God listens to us because of His love for us. By being a good listener, we are becoming more Christ-like. Consider the following:

- "This you know, my beloved brethren, but everyone must be quick to hear, slow to speak and slow to anger (James 1:19).
- "The eyes of the Lord are on the righteous, and his ears are attentive to their cry" (Psalm 34:15).

- "Let the wise hear and increase in learning, and the one who understands obtain guidance" (Proverbs 1:5).

In addition to specific scripture, we have a biblical pattern of active listening for us to learn from and apply when supporting sisters in need. Note the following:

Esther: The book of Esther teaches us the importance of active listening. Esther is a Jew who also becomes the new queen to King Ahasuerus. Haman, who was an advisor to the King, orders everyone to bow down to him as a sign of respect. Mordecai, who was a father figure to Esther (Esther 2:7), refuses to bow down to Haman. Haman plots to have all Jewish subjects killed. Esther eventually reveals the plans to the King and her identity as a Jew, and the King has Haman killed.

In Esther 4, we see a conversation between Mordecai and Esther unfold, which completely affected the future of the Jewish nation. Esther was concerned for her own safety if she went to the King and revealed that she was a Jew. She listened attentively to Mordecai as he pleaded with her to understand that the hope of the Jewish nation was on her shoulders. She listened carefully when he suggested in Esther 4:14, "For if you keep silent at this time, relief and deliverance will rise for the Jews from another place, but you and your father's house will perish. And who knows whether you have not come to the kingdom for such a time as this?"

For us to support sisters, we must place a priority on listening completely. We must be present to listen to the other person's feelings, pain, circumstances, and opinions. We never know how or when God will work through us to help others, and it all begins with listening. [3]

Samuel: In 1 Samuel 3:1–10, we read of the account of Samuel in the tabernacle and God calling out to him. Samuel is sleeping in the temple itself when he is awakened by the sound of his name being called. He runs to Eli. Eli tells Samuel he did not call him and sends him back to bed. It happens again with the same result. Only when Samuel answers and says, "Speak, for your servant hears," does God answer him. Samuel heard God calling his name previously, so he was hearing, but he was not listening. It is quite possible to hear someone without listening. Samuel heard God calling him, but God did not give Samuel further instruction until he was ready to listen. When we are supporting sisters in need, it does not help to just hear their struggles, we must also listen carefully to what they are saying. Many times, you will need to "read between the lines" to understand the source of her struggles and pain. Active listening will assist you in supporting sisters.

Mary: Luke 10:38–42 records the account of Jesus going to the home of Mary and Martha. This account is familiar to us as it shows how Martha was busy with the preparations for welcoming Jesus while Mary did not help her. Instead of helping Martha, Mary sat at the feet of Jesus and listened to Him. She knew she had a unique opportunity to listen to Jesus's teachings, and she did not want that time to pass. Mary listened intently to what Jesus was saying. Active listening is about being present in the moment, focusing on the other person, and not being distracted by other things. Many times, we get so distracted with "things" that we do not stop to listen, and we have missed the opportunity.

Jesus and Active Listening

Sisters who are struggling many times are looking for someone who will listen to them. Jesus knew the best way to minister to people was by simply listening. Jesus is our best example of someone who mastered the skill of active listening. Consider the following examples where Jesus employed active listening to support others who were struggling.

The Wedding at Cana: The account of the Wedding at Cana is described in John 2. The wine had run out, and there was no wine to serve to the guests at the wedding. In Jewish tradition, this would have been very embarrassing for the hosts of the wedding. Jesus's mother told Him, "They have no wine." He could tell by His mother's tone of voice that the lack of wine was causing stress. Jesus listened not only to her words but to the emotion that was underlying. He listened for a sense of urgency in her voice, which could indicate pain and stress. Throughout His ministry, Jesus listened in a way that helped Him identify a person's need during their struggles. Although He had more pressing thoughts of what was to come (John 2:4), He gave her His full attention and supported her in a time of need.

The Samaritan Woman at the Well: Jesus was willing to see the woman at the well for someone whose soul needed to be saved. We know from John 4:9, "You are a Jew, and I am a Samaritan woman. How can you ask me for a drink? (For Jews do not associate with Samaritans)." Jesus risked being accused of becoming ceremonially unclean if He used a drinking vessel handled by a Samaritan since the Jews held that all Samaritans were unclean. Jesus knew her background, but He was able to look past her home life for the sake of her soul. He listened to her, had an important conversation with her, and made an impact on her that changed her life!

Those Who Were Hurting: When we see sisters, especially our older sisters, who are in physical pain, this is when they need our greatest support. They need to know that they are loved and appreciated during their senior years. Jesus spent a great deal of time listening to people who were physically hurting. Consider the following examples:

∼Those who were sick and oppressed by demons (Mark 1:32–34).

∼Ten Lepers (Luke 17:11–19).

∼Woman Who Bled Twelve Years (Mark 5:25–34).

Jesus not only listened to specific problems, but He also showed interest in physical healing, as well as emotional, social, and spiritual restoration of the person. As we support our sisters, we want to always support them in a way that will bring them closer to Christ.

Why Is Active Listening Important When Supporting Sisters?

Listening to others is the most basic form of communication we have. Listening to sisters who need support will start a dialogue that will hopefully lead to comfort. Active listening provides a safe environment for a sister, allows us to minister to her needs, and also gives her a voice. Not only do we have a clear biblical pattern for active listening, but when we support our sisters through active listening, we provide a safe environment in which they can share their struggles. We validate her struggles and concerns while learning the best way to support her. We demonstrate a Christ-like behavior by counting others more significant than ourselves (Philippians 2:3 and also looking at the interests of others (Philippians 2:4).

Listening to a sister who is in need could be the most important thing that you can do for her. Many times, sisters will know the solution to their problem or the behavior they need to change to make the struggle manageable. She just needs someone she can trust to simply listen. She may not expect nor desire anything from you in return but to listen.

When sisters are in pain, they may feel that they are not being heard. It is possible that their family members and/or friends are not listening to their concerns. We always want to provide an avenue for our sisters to be heard. This will help her work through her emotions and help her to heal.

Practical Ways to Demonstrate Active Listening

Now that we have established the importance of active listening, let us discover practical ways to demonstrate active listening. From our definition of active listening earlier in the chapter, notice some key phrases: preparing to listen, verbal and nonverbal messages, and appropriate feedback.

- Prepare to Listen: Always make sure you are in the right mindset to listen to a sister in need. Pray before you begin that God will give you wisdom and the words to say that will best help the sister. You want to make sure you are physically facing the sister. You might need to move furniture around, and that is fine. It is better not to have a barrier between you and her, such as a desk or table. Have as much of an open posture with your body as you can (do not cross your arms over your body). An open posture from you will create a sense of support, too. Make sure you always hold eye contact with the sister. Many times, sisters who need support will look away at particularly emotional conversations, and that is fine. But you want to always make sure you are making eye contact with her. Always "lean in" to the conversation. This posture will create a sense of focus, attention, and comfort for the sister. Always remove outside distractions, especially cell phones.

You do not want to give the sister the impression that something else is more important to you than listening to her struggles.

- Observing Verbal and Nonverbal Messages: When supporting a sister, it is important for you to notice the verbal and nonverbal cues she may be giving. You want to make sure you are aware of how she is responding. Examples of verbal cues include her tone of voice, if she is using words that let you know she is frustrated or tired, or if she is ready to share what her struggle really is. Nonverbal cues include her body language, such as hand gestures, eye rolls, and facial expressions. Is she distracted by looking around the room, noticing her phone, etc.? Is she rubbing her eyes or her temples? This could be a sign that she is upset, or she might have a stress headache. It is helpful for you to "read the room" and notice any of these verbal and nonverbal cues. Depending on how she is responding will determine the next steps for support.

- Provide Appropriate Feedback: Appropriate feedback to a sister you are supporting is crucial. When sisters seek support, they look to you for love, guidance, and godly solutions to their struggles. As we have discussed earlier in this chapter, they may be looking for someone to listen to them. It is helpful for you to nod your head in agreement as this will give affirmation of what the sister is sharing. Offer comfort when needed, and rather than giving answers you deem to be correct, support and influence her in a manner where she will seek God's guidance. After you have established a relationship of trust, solutions will be easier to find if they are wanted.

When I was in graduate school, I had the privilege of learning from Dr. Bill Bagents and Dr. Rosemary Snodgrass. In their book *Counseling for Church Leaders: A Practical Guide*, they discussed the importance of listening when supporting others. The following is adapted from Bagents and Snodgrass.

In order to help and support someone in need, the ultimate goal is to have an open dialogue of effective conversation. A few suggestions to accomplish this:

- Listen to Understand their perspective and the issue at hand. When my son was in high school, he would come to me and say, "I need to talk to you about something, but I don't need you to fix it, I just need you to listen." No matter how well we know the sister or the problem they are dealing with, we need to listen. If you speculate and form an opinion beforehand, because "I have an idea of what is going on," can be dangerous and unproductive. When we share our thoughts, feelings, and perspectives with each other, this builds a deeper bond and hopefully a trusting relationship.
- Strive for True Dialogue. This includes having a conversation while offering support. Focus on the conversation by listening and responding to what the person is saying at that moment—do not think ahead about how you will respond to something that has not even been discussed. Keep an open mind and strive to influence each other.
- Silence is Golden. If you do not know what to say, just do not say anything. Silence during a

conversation will allow for reflection and time for processing the next steps. You want to give the sister time to determine in which direction she wants to proceed.[4]

Active listening is critical in all relationships. But we always want to seek to listen and understand another sister's perspective when she needs support. We see examples from scripture of active listening and how it is effectively shown. We need to study these scriptures and learn from them. Active listening is a skill that can be developed and is needed when supporting sisters who are struggling. The more you practice the skill of active listening, the easier it will become. Katherine Whitehorn once said, "A good listener is a good talker with a sore throat." We do not want to have a sore throat in order to be a good active listener!

Questions for Discussion

1. Why do you believe active listening is so difficult for many to master?
2. In what ways can we encourage each other to be better active listeners?
3. Name some personal reminders that you could incorporate in your life to help you to become a better listener.

Chapter 6

Tool 3: Demonstrating Empathy

Empathy is seeing with the eyes of another, listening with the ears of another and feeling with the heart of another.

— *Alfred Adler*

WHEN YOU THINK OF EMPATHY, the woman known to the world as Mother Teresa may come to mind. As a Catholic nun known as Saint Teresa of Calcutta, she founded the Missionaries of Charity in 1950. Throughout her life, she was well known for her work with the poor, orphans, and people dying from AIDS, leprosy, and tuberculosis. In her early life, she was fascinated by the stories and lives of missionaries. She decided at age twelve to commit to a religious life. In 1946, she heeded the call to serve the poor of India. Her life's work personified empathy.

Empathy is not just about helping those who are less fortunate. Demonstrating empathy for others is an important quality in all aspects of life–even in the business world. *Harvard Business Review* highlighted the fact that CEOs believe that empathy and empathy training are important to the workforce. CEO of Apple, Tim Cook, addressed MIT graduates in 2017. He stated, "People will try to convince you that you should keep empathy out of your career. Don't accept this false premise."[1] The article goes on to state that empathetic workplaces tend to enjoy stronger collaboration, less stress, and greater morale. When empathy is demonstrated to others, no matter the environment, there is a strong sense of urgency to support one another.

The Roof

If you ever find yourself lost in the woods and need a place of safety, survival experts say one of the first things to do is to build some sort of shelter. You will need protection from the elements and also from predators. A roof on our houses also provides that same protection. Just as the roof on the house acts as protection, empathy will serve as protection when supporting sisters.

When you demonstrate empathy, you understand and share the feelings of what a person is going through. This empathetic affirmation will let our sisters know they are protected, they are not alone in what they feel, and they are supported. Since we all develop and demonstrate empathy at varying degrees, this chapter will guide us through biblical examples of empathy, offer practical ways to demonstrate empathy to sisters who are in need and highlight ways of how you can develop empathy.

What Is Empathy?

Empathy is the

> action of understanding, being aware of, being sensitive to,
> and vicariously experiencing the feelings, thoughts, and expe-
> rience of another of either the past or present without having
> the feelings, thoughts, and experience fully communicated in
> an objectively explicit manner.[2]

Simply stated, empathy is the ability to feel another person's emotions and share in their emotional experiences. When supporting sisters, it is important to see the struggle from their perspective. This will enable you to understand why they feel the way they do. There is an old saying, "Walk a mile in my shoes." This is what empathy is all about. We all come from different experiences and backgrounds, and we do not always react to situations the same. Therefore, when offering support, we all need to understand different perspectives and place ourselves in the situation. If applicable, it might be appropriate to let your sister know you have the same struggles. We are all broken, and we all need Christ. The revelation of your strug-gles will bring about a feeling of comfort, and the sister will know she is not alone. We want to offer hope and guidance that will support our sister to make godly decisions and bring her closer to Christ.

Demonstrating empathy, on the other hand, may not always be straightforward. It is often uncomfortable for you to listen to the struggles of a sister in Christ. These struggles are often heartbreaking, and if you are like me, you want to "fix" the situation. But it is not that easy. When you are dealing with sisters, and there is sin involved (whether it is personal sin or sin from another that is causing the difficulty), you must give support and guidance to her and help her to come to her own resolution of the situation at hand. Your active listening skills will be needed to support the sister, and these skills can become powerful! Carl Rogers, a psychologist, said, "We think we listen, but very rarely do we listen with real understanding, true empathy. Yet listening, of this very special kind, is one of the most potent forces for change that I know."[3] When she feels heard and understood, only then will she begin to heal.

Always remember, in order to be empathetic, you do not need to have the exact same experiences or pain as someone else, but you must be able to understand and acknowledge their pain in a loving way. Empathetic people are able to show love, kindness, and care, regardless of a lack of shared circumstances. In other words, it is the ability to understand and share the feelings and suffering of another.

You might be wondering, "Can empathy be developed?" We all know people who are naturally empathetic and some who are not. But yes, empathy can be developed. During our lives, we all move through stages of empathy development. Toddlers, for example, will often show signs of early empathetic development by the way they treat others. They will often apologize, offer help, and show concern for others. They will also begin to mimic forms of empathy they see from others. A person will develop different degrees of empathy depending on circumstances and life experiences as they become adults. In extreme circumstances, someone might develop little or no empathy for others.[4] But through the examples the Bible gives us, we can learn to become more empathetic to our sisters who are struggling.

Demonstrating empathy is an ability that all Christians should embody. It is particularly imperative for those who want to support sisters to be empathetic. Empathy is important to demonstrate at the beginning of the helping relationship and will result in a connection for the helping to take place.[5] When we support sisters, we must first seek to understand and then envision ourselves in the situation. We must be willing and able to step into her emotions, feelings, and circumstances. Jesus himself personified empathy. "Jesus is portrayed as having the ability to understand and put himself in the position of those to whom he ministered. He wanted to experience what they experienced so he could better minister to them."[6] When we support sisters who are struggling, we should always follow the example of Christ.

Empathy in Scripture

The Bible points to scripture that illustrates the role empathy should play in our lives as Christians. Scripture centered around bearing one another's burdens are seen in Galatians 6:2–3, 1 Thessalonians 5:11, Hebrews 10:24–25, 1 Peter 4:10, and Romans 12:15. We also see the importance of being considerate of others as seen in Philippians 2:2–4, 1 Corinthians 10:24, 1 Corinthians 10:33, and Romans 15:1. We are comforted to know that God is empathetic. Consider the following:

- "You have kept count of my tossings; put my tears in your bottle. Are they not in your book?" (Psalm 56:8)
- "For he knows our frame; he remembers that we are dust" (Psalm 103:14).

God knows each and every struggle and emotion we have. He created us and knows our struggles beforehand. As Christians, this is a great comfort, and we know through the avenue of prayer we can cast our anxieties on Him because He cares for us (1 Peter 5:7).

Jesus and Empathy

Jesus showed empathy to others throughout his ministry. He walked in flesh (John 1:14), and He experienced every human emotion. Hebrews 4:15 provides comfort: "For we do not have a high priest who is unable to empathize with our weaknesses, but we have one who has been tempted in every way, just as we are, yet he did not sin." Throughout His earthly ministry, Jesus provides the example of empathy, and as Christians, we can rejoice that He has complete empathy for the struggles we have in our lives today.

Let us notice examples of how Jesus demonstrated empathy to others who were in need:

- In Luke 13:10–17, we see Jesus teaching in the synagogue on a Sabbath. There was a woman in the synagogue who was crippled and had been in that condition for eighteen years. Jesus saw her and healed her. According to the Pharisees, healing on the Sabbath was unlawful, and they were upset that Jesus was healing on that day. Not only did Jesus heal her, but He also demonstrated empathy toward her. He defied the law of the Pharisees and made her whole. Now, Jesus did not suffer from being crippled as the woman did, but He still demonstrated empathy toward her, and He wanted to heal her pain.
- In Matthew 9:35–38, we have the account of Jesus teaching in the synagogues and healing crowds of people. When Jesus saw the people, His heart went

out to them. Scripture tells us they were "harassed
and helpless." Jesus demonstrated empathy toward
them because He wanted all people to experience
His love because they were "like a sheep without a
shepherd."

- We see many examples in scripture of Jesus
demonstrating empathy to women. Because of the
societal structure in the first century, women were
seen as inferior and subordinate to men. But Jesus
did not hold this view. He treated women with
respect and kindness. Consider these examples of
empathy: In Luke 7:36–50, we read the account of
the woman who we know was a sinner. But she
wiped Jesus's feet with her hair and anointed them
with ointment. She came to Jesus in search of
redemption, and He did not turn her away. In Luke
7:11–17, we read of the account of the widow of
Nain. This widow was overcome with sorrow
because her only son had died, and she was
childless. Jesus did not overlook her or turn the
other way. Jesus raised the boy from the dead and
gave the boy back to the widow.

Jesus extends empathy to us today. Despite Jesus being
God in the flesh, He never acted prideful, superior, or indif-
ferent to the people. Jesus always showed love to everyone He
came in contact with. Empathy is an extension of love, and as
Christians, we are to demonstrate empathy to those in need.

Why Is It Important to Demonstrate Empathy When Supporting Sisters?

The obvious answer as to why we should demonstrate empathy when we support sisters is because Jesus has given us a pattern to do just that. If we study the examples that the inspired scriptures provide for us and apply those, we will become more Christ-like, which will, in turn, help us to further the kingdom. But when supporting sisters who are struggling, demonstrating empathy goes deeper. It is about encouraging the sister to feel comfortable enough to share struggles that are keeping her from living the life Christ wants her to live. The kind of life where she will be productive in her household, in her secular work, and in her congregation. Demonstrating empathy toward sisters who are struggling provides protection to give them the confidence to seek support.

Practical Ways to Demonstrate Empathy

Now that we have established a biblical pattern for demonstrating empathy and have determined why it is important to support sisters, let us consider practical ways we can show empathy.

Make Eye Contact

The first step in demonstrating empathy to a sister is to make eye contact. This is part of active listening that was discussed earlier. When you make direct eye contact with her, she will know that she has your full attention and that you are focused on what she is saying.

Be Aware

Notice how your sisters are doing. Engage in conversation with them if you get a sense they need a friend. They may open up to you if they are struggling with something specific, and you can let them know that you care about their situation and that you would be glad to listen and help in any way that you can. When we go out of the way to check on our sisters, they will see empathy is directed towards them. As Christians, we are commanded to love our neighbor and have great love for fellow believers (Matthew 22:39; 1 Peter 4:8). Part of this love is to show empathy and support our sisters in times of struggle. This is why it is so important to maintain awareness of our sisters, as it will aid in supporting sisters.

Meet The Need

When a sister seeks our support, you may be able to help her in a way that will alleviate her pain. Concerns and struggles she has may be remedied with the right kind of support. If you have the ability to understand and help with the need, you should. That is what Christians do. On the other hand, many struggles are not "fixable" by the one offering support. The best way to support her is to let the sister know you love her, God loves her, and there is hope.

Mourn With Them

There is a popular saying, "It gives me all the feels," which is slang for an overwhelming emotional reaction. I cannot think of a better way to demonstrate empathy to our sisters than to cry with them when they are sad. When you cry with them, you are saying, "I am so sorry. I understand this hurts. I want to be here for you." They will see that you are looking at things from their eyes because you are feeling what they are feeling in the moment. This "mourning" is not just about the loss of a loved one. It could be any loss, such as the loss of a relationship, the loss of a job, the loss of what the future could have been, the loss of a soul, etc. As sisters in Christ, we are connected on a different level than our friends outside the body of Christ. We know that our home is not here, but we have to endure the world as it is.

Prayer

Praying is one of the best things you can do with someone who is struggling. When you pray for someone, they know you care about them and that can be a source of comfort. Pray specifically about their need and that God would give them peace through the trials that they are going through. Pray that God will be with them through it all and use you to help them. We will discuss the importance of prayer when supporting sisters in a later chapter.

All of these ways to show empathy can be summed up with 1 Corinthians 13:7, "Love bears all things, believes all things, hopes all things, endures all things." If you love someone like this, they will definitely know that you are trying to see things from their point of view, and your empathy will comfort them.

How to Develop Empathy

Being empathetic comes naturally for some of us. To others, it may not. But our ability to be empathetic to others is not fixed; it can be developed. Consider the following ways to help you develop empathy.

Be Curious

When you spend time with sisters, especially ones you do not know very well, ask them about themselves, how they are, and how life is going. You will want to find the balance of not appearing too overbearing or giving the impression you are being nosey but rather showing a genuine interest in them. Most people are fond of discussing themselves, and this will give you a great insight into what, if anything, they are struggling with. Notice what makes them passionate, happy, or sad. This could be the beginning of building trust in the relationship.

Step Out of Your Comfort Zone

When you step out of your comfort zone, you become vulnerable. Learn a new hobby, take a class about something you would like to know more about, and get to know people with whom you might not have much in common. All of these things will encourage humility, which is helpful in demonstrating empathy. (And when you are outside your comfort zone, you might have the opportunity to show God's love as well.)

Examine Your Biases

We all have biases to some extent, and sometimes those biases may cause us to judge others on the way they look or how they live. Peter discusses this in Acts 10:34–35. "So Peter opened his mouth and said: "Truly I understand that God shows no partiality, but in every nation anyone who fears him and does what is right is acceptable to him." When we are biased against someone, it can have a negative impact on our capacity for empathy. In order to make sure we do not have biases, we need to get to know one another better. Have a conversation about what is important in their lives, and see what similarities and interests are shared. And then become aware of biases you may have held before you got to know them better.

Walk in Their Shoes

Developing empathy centers around getting to know others on a deeper level. To be empathetic, you need to understand what it is like for people in other situations. Discover how they live, what kind of work they do, or what their future dreams are. Building relationships that are meaningful will allow you to understand their concerns and their hopes. Seek to understand their upbringing as a child, and this will allow you to understand the perspectives they have as an adult. As sisters in Christ, we should all strive to know each other on a deeper and more meaningful level.

Demonstrating empathy can be hard for some of us. But, showing a sister that you have the ability to understand her experiences in a sincere manner will help to ease her pain. Examples of empathy are throughout scripture, but in today's world, it may be difficult to demonstrate. We all live busy lives, but we must never be too busy to support our sisters who are struggling. As Christians, we always want to strive to do God's will and be empathetic to our sisters in Christ. By being aware of others' struggles and making ourselves available to offer support, we are demonstrating the love that Christ has for all of us.

Questions for Discussion

1. Why does it seem to be difficult for many to demonstrate empathy to others?
2. What can we do as Christian women to make sure empathy is developed in those we influence?
3. Reflect on what biases you may have on others. What can you do to personally minimize those biases?

Chapter 7

Tool 4: Demonstrating a Christ-Like Love

Love is unselfishly choosing for another's highest good.

— C.S. Lewis

LOVE IS a subject that everyone knows something about. We know of the love of parents for their children, the love between a husband and wife, the love between friends, and the love that Christ has for His church. We all want to love and be loved. We know from scripture that God is love (1 John 4:8), and as Christians, we all strive to demonstrate a Christ-like love to others every day. Sisters who are struggling, particularly, need to feel the love of their sisters in Christ. We want to support our sisters out of our love for them, our love for Christ, and His love for us (John 15:12). This chapter will discuss biblical examples of Christ-like love and how to effectively demonstrate Christ-like love when supporting sisters.

The Walls

When you are building a structure, walls are needed to provide additional support for the structure. Without walls, the structure will not remain upright and will fall. Demonstrating a Christ-like love to sisters who are struggling will function as these walls and will provide that additional support they need. While we are commanded to show Christ-like love for one another (John 13:34–35), sisters who are struggling will appreciate this specific support. Theodore Roosevelt once said, "People don't care how much we know until they know how much we care." Once Christ-like love is demonstrated, this will begin a relationship of trust and care that will provide comfort to those who are hurting.

What Is Christ-Like Love?

Throughout scripture, we see different types of love. You may be familiar with and have studied the definitions: eros (romantic love), storge (familial love), philia (brotherly love), and agape (God's love for mankind). Christ-like love is agape love. This love is considered the highest form of love as it is selfless, sacrificial, and unconditional. God demonstrated this love to all sinners by sending Jesus to die on the cross (John 3:16). Jesus demonstrated this love to all sinners when He died on the cross. As we see in 1 John 4:10, Christ-like love is sacrificial, and it is about giving, serving, and commitment. To support sisters, you must be willing to give (your time, wisdom, and, to an extent, your emotions and thoughts), service, and support. Christ-like love is unique; it is selfless.

Perhaps the most notable scripture that demonstrates Christ-like love is found in Luke 15:1–7. Jesus tells the Parable of the Lost Sheep, where he highlights the importance of finding just one sheep. He notes in verse seven, "There will be more joy in heaven over one sinner who repents than over ninety-nine righteous persons who need no repentance." There is not a situation or circumstance that God will not help us with. This promise is made in 1 Corinthians 10:13 that He will not let us be tempted to the point that it is unbearable, and He will provide us with a way to endure anything Satan has in mind. The love that our Father has for us is immeasurable. As we support sisters who are hurting, this type of selfless, unwavering love is what they need the most from us!

How Is Christ-Like Love Demonstrated in Scripture?

All throughout the New Testament, we see numerous examples of Jesus demonstrating love to others. He did so in various ways, including acts of service, showing forgiveness, and the ultimate sacrifice of His death on the cross. Let us notice these ways:

Service

When you think of Christ-like love, the example of Jesus and His service to others comes to mind. Consider the following ways Jesus served:

- One of the most notable acts of service is the account of Jesus washing the feet of His disciples in John 13. This is an unusual act of service in that the washing of feet was normally the job of the household servants, not the Son. But Jesus wanted to demonstrate love to His disciples by serving them, which is the same pattern Christians maintain when we support our sisters.

- Jesus had a special love for the "least of these," especially the children. We read of Him raising Jarius's daughter in Mark 5. Jarius was a ruler at the synagogue and had approached Jesus because his daughter was ill–to the point of death. Jesus raised her. Women who are suffering need healing. Jesus, the Great Physician, will heal those in need. When we support women, we demonstrate the love Jesus has for them, and this will aid in their healing.
- When Jesus fed the five thousand, He saw a need, and because of His love for those men, women, and children, they ate and were satisfied. When we see a need, especially for sisters who are struggling, we can show love to them by meeting that need if we are able.
- Teaching is one of the most important acts of service one can do. Jesus taught to anyone He encountered. Because of His love for mankind, through his teaching, He was able to offer an eternity in heaven to all who were willing to accept and obey.

Forgiveness

Jesus speaks about the importance of forgiving others during His ministry. In Matthew 18:21–22, Peter is asking how many times he should forgive a brother who has sinned against him. Jesus said to him, "I do not say to you seven times, but seventy-seven times." In Matthew 6:14, Jesus speaks plainly that we must forgive others so God will forgive us of our trespasses. Jesus provides us with a clear pattern of forgiveness, and as Christians, we must follow that pattern. But the most important example we have of Jesus's forgiveness centers around the cross. As Jesus was hanging on the cross, He prayed, "Forgive them for they know not what they do" (Luke 23:34). As He was betrayed and suffering, he demonstrated the ultimate act of love by asking God to forgive those who were responsible. This was an intentional and conscious choice made by Jesus. What an example that is to us!

Sacrifice

While Jesus was on the earth, He preached sacrifice. We have numerous examples of His sacrifice for us. Notice the following examples:

- When Jesus left heaven and came to earth to walk with men and became a servant, He sacrificed His own godly status and the divine privilege of heaven. He emptied Himself so that He could redeem mankind and fulfill the Father's plan of salvation. Consider the words Paul wrote to the church in Phillipi: "Who, though He was in the form of God, did not count equality with God a thing to be grasped, but emptied himself, by taking the form of a servant, being born in the likeness of men. And being found in human form, He humbled himself by becoming obedient to the point of death, even death on a cross" (Philippians 2:6–8).

- When Jesus left heaven for earth, He sacrificed His comfort. During His ministry, He was spoken to disrespectfully, mocked because of His name, and had to depend on others to have necessities such as food and a place to sleep. He was rejected by the very people He came to save. Paul writes in 2 Corinthians 8:9, "For you know the grace of our Lord Jesus Christ, that though he was rich, yet for

your sake he became poor, so that you by his
poverty might become rich."

- The greatest sacrifice Jesus gave was His life. He
  had to endure the suffering on the cross, knowing
  He was guilty of no crime. He watched as His
  mother and friends grieved as they witnessed the
  cruel punishment of the cross. He understood that
  suffering had to occur to carry out God's plan of
  salvation. This sacrifice of Jesus is the perfect
  example of His love for us. We should strive to
  follow this example every day of our lives, as we see
  in Ephesians 5:2, "and walk in love, as Christ loved
  us and gave himself up for us, a fragrant offering
  and sacrifice to God."

The Importance of Demonstrating Christ-like Love to Support Sisters

All of us need love. A classic song from the Beatles reminds us
that "love is all you need." From the moment babies are born,
they need to feel love and be touched. Research has shown that
babies who have not bonded properly with their parents, who
have not been touched, and shown love, will more than likely
suffer emotionally and socially as they become adults. This
bonding between parent and child is known as Skin-to-Skin
Contact, where the newborn baby needs to feel the touch of
another.[1] Love, even from the earliest days of life, is funda-
mental to our existence for us to become well-adjusted,
emotionally, and socially strong adults.

As I have supported women over the years, many women
simply do not feel loved. They lack the love they need from
their husband, parents, children, or friends. This has led to feelings of unworthiness, insecurity, and lack of self-confidence.

When sisters struggle, they need to feel love, security, and hope. As we support sisters, let us demonstrate the Christ-like love we see in scripture (Romans 5:8), which will help lead to their healing.

Practical Ways to Demonstrate Christ- like Love

We want to demonstrate Christ-like love in practical ways to sisters who are struggling. These practical ways will serve as an example for sisters as they struggle and as they eventually heal from their pain. Consider the following:

- Extend Grace: The Hebrew writer tells us of the importance of when we are in need, to find grace. "Let us then with confidence draw near to the throne of grace that we may receive mercy and find grace to help in time of need" (Hebrews 4:16). We can approach God in prayer in our time of need. As Christians, we have grace extended to us through Christ, and a wonderful and comforting gift that is! When a sister is suffering, it will provide her comfort to remind her of this special gift. As sisters, we can also extend grace to her by being present and walking alongside her. Many times, when we struggle, we need someone who will give us time to come to a godly resolution. Make sure you give the struggling sister that time with patience, understanding, kindness, and empathy. For someone who is struggling, these things will go a long way in the support process. Remind her of 1 Peter 5:10: "And after you have suffered a little while, the God of all grace, who has called you to his eternal glory in Christ, will himself restore, confirm, strengthen, and establish you."

- Model Forgiveness: Sisters who have been hurt will sometimes find it hard to forgive. They will need time to heal from their pain, and forgiveness will be part of that healing. But they will need space and time to forgive when they are ready. As you support her, always model forgiveness, and gently remind her (at an appropriate time) that we are to forgive as God has forgiven us (Ephesians 4:31–32).
- Sacrifice Comfortability: When we demonstrate Christ-like love, we are making a sacrifice for another person. These sacrifices come in a variety of forms. You will find yourself thinking about her struggles, which might make you feel sad or angry because sin, by her or someone else, has caused her pain. She may reveal to you situations that are hard for you to comprehend. These situations may make you feel uncomfortable, but it is always important to let the sister know you love her and will offer support in any way you can.
- Share Your Talents: We are stewards of what God has blessed us with, and as such, we need to use our talents to show God's love to our sisters. When supporting sisters, think about the talents God has given you and how you could make her situation easier. Examples include making a meal, babysitting her children, helping her with her housekeeping, and engaging in a weekly Bible study that focuses on God's promises, faithfulness, and love. Think outside of the box and determine which talent might best support her.

- Speak Truth: Sharing and speaking truth is one of the best things we can do for a sister who is in need. Be mindful of 1 Corinthians 13:6, where Paul tells us that love does not rejoice in wrongdoing but rejoices in the truth. Sharing the truth of Christ will always be the right thing to do. Always speak in kindness and love so that she will see God's faithfulness and hope.

- Check on Her Often: Send a quick text or make a phone call just to let her know you are thinking of her. Whether she is struggling or not, she likes to know that her sisters are thinking of her. That text or phone call might just come at a time when she needs it the most! A simple gesture of reminder of God's love and hope for the future will go a long way in the healing process. Always remind her she has a positive path forward, and God will provide (1 Corinthians 10:13).

- Tangible Reminders: You might suggest she keep a journal of God's blessings she sees in her life. Encourage her to think back to a time when God providentially carried her through a valley. This will enable her to remember that God is faithful to His children. She might also like to start a Joy Box. This is a box of anything that brings her joy. For example, favorite scriptures, pictures of someone who is important to her, a card that someone wrote to her, etc. This will also serve as a reminder to her of God's love and the people He has placed in her life.

Life on earth is not easy. I have a dear sister who always reminds me, "Life is hard, it's not heaven!" We understand life from our perspective. The facts of a situation do not change, but our perspectives can. Because God has given us a sound mind and discernment (Hosea 14:9, 2 Timothy 1:7, Romans 12:2), we show sisters Christ-like love during their struggles. We all face struggles, and we know when we do, God's faithfulness is constant. Hopefully, we will grow spiritually in the midst of the struggles, which, in turn, will draw us closer to Him. Some sisters may not feel the growth during their struggles, but prayerfully, when they look back at that moment in their lives, they will see that God carried them through!

Questions for Discussion

1. In what ways do you demonstrate Christ-like love in your everyday life? Think outside of those in your congregation.
2. If you struggle with forgiving others, reflect on why. Engage in Bible study about the importance of forgiveness. Seek out sisters who can keep you accountable as you work through the struggle.
3. Reflect on your talents and determine how they might have changed in our current season of life. Determine which of these talents could be best used to demonstrate Christ-like love to sisters who are in need.

PART 3: Making a House a Home
(Being an Effective Supporter)

Chapter 8

Tool 5: Effective Communication – Part 1

In many ways, effective communication begins with mutual respect and inspires, encouraging others to do their best.

— Zig Ziglar

Lighting

EFFECTIVE COMMUNICATION IS essential when supporting sisters. If we cannot convey our words in an effective manner, supporting sisters will become difficult. Communication is more than having a conversation with someone. This chapter will highlight how to effectively communicate using verbal and nonverbal cues. Asking the right kinds of questions is equally as important as learning to communicate through verbal and nonverbal methods, and the next chapter will focus on which types of questions to ask and why that is important when supporting sisters.

As we notice areas of importance in building a house, lighting inside a house is at the top of the list. Lighting within a house allows us to see our path forward, but it also allows us to see obstacles that might cause us to fall. Lighting provides a way out of darkness. Effective communication (verbal and nonverbal), like lighting, highlights a path of hope to engage with sisters who need support when they feel like they are in darkness while also revealing obstacles that may keep them from healing.

What Is Effective Communication?

The earliest forms of communication include fire and smoke signals, different beats on a drum, symbols on cave walls, hand gestures, acting, and dancing. The Sumerians and Egyptians were the first to develop systems of writing in Ancient Mesopotamia. Ancient man determined it was important to develop a way to communicate with each other. Today, we have multiple ways to communicate by using computers, smartphones, and Alexa. Verbal communication is essential to our everyday lives. It is also essential when we support sisters who are struggling.

According to Indeed.com, "Verbal communication refers to the use of language to convey information."[1] Verbal communication encompasses not only how you speak but also what you say. Effective communication, including verbal communication, is the foundation to which we can support one another. Verbal communication will be the most common form of communication you will use in supporting a sister. It is vital that good, effective communication skills are learned and practiced.

Nonverbal communication can be just as important as verbal communication. Although we discussed some of these nonverbal skills in Chapter 5, they warrant highlighting here. Remember to maintain eye contact, keep an open posture with your body while leaning into the conversation, nod your head in agreement, if appropriate, to show validation and encouragement, and control facial expressions.

Learning to effectively communicate using verbal and nonverbal communication will help you build a rapport and build a trusting relationship with the sister you are supporting. Effective communication will help to define reality, to gain clarity, and allow for the organization of our thoughts to begin to see a path forward.

Where Does Effective Communication Begin?

Jesus reveals to us that effective communication begins in the heart. In Matthew 12:34–37, He emphasizes,

> You brood of vipers! How can you speak good when you are evil? For out of the abundance of the heart the mouth speaks. The good person out of his good treasure brings forth good, and the evil person out of his evil treasure brings forth evil. I tell you, on the day of judgment people will give account for every careless word they speak, for by your words you will be justified, and by your words you will be condemned.

We must guard our hearts because our words and actions flow from our hearts. Paul David Tripp, in his book *War on Words: Getting to the Heart of Our Communication Struggles,* said, "Word problems reveal heart problems. The people and situations around us do not make us say what we say, they are only the occasion for our hearts to reveal themselves in words."[2] The way you communicate will reflect what you treasure in your heart. King Solomon also discussed the heart in Proverbs 4:23, saying, "Keep your heart with all vigilance, for from it flow the springs of life," meaning what we treasure in our heart will drive our desires, and that drives our choices. Although effective communication begins in the heart, we want to always make sure we understand the responsibility we have when we communicate effectively with a sister who is struggling. You never know what word or words you might say that could make the difference in her life. We always want to reflect Christ in everything we do or say, and effective communication plays a vital role (Colossians 3:17; Proverbs 10:21, 16:21, 24).

Paul, in Ephesians 4:1–2, addresses how we as Christians should communicate with each other within the body of Christ. In verse one, Paul urges the church in Ephesus to "walk in a manner worthy of the calling to which you have been called." What a great responsibility we as Christians have. As Christians, we know we can never do or say enough to warrant Jesus's death on the cross. But through our communication, we can always remember that sacrifice and make sure we always reflect Christ. Let us notice key phrases in verse 2:

- Be Humble: (verse 2) When supporting sisters in need, we want to make sure we show humility. Meaning we put our own interests above the sister we are helping. Christ, throughout his life on earth, showed us examples of humility, and that is the pattern we should use. When supporting sisters who are in need, our motives must be unselfish, which will be reflected in our communication. We read in James 3:16, "For where jealousy and selfish ambition exist, there will be disorder and every vile practice." Our personal motives or agendas must be set aside, and only seek her interests, and your support will draw her closer to Christ. When our motive is to look to the interests of others, we honor God, and effective communication ensues.

- Be Gentle: (verse 2) The sister you are supporting will most likely be in a fragile, emotional state. Use words that are not harsh, judgmental, or demeaning. We want to offer her hope for the future and remind her that God will see her through the situation.
- Be Patient: (verse 2) Remember the sister is seeking help because of some difficulty in her life. This could be caused by her own sin, temptation, or the sins of someone else. This is not the time to be abrupt, sarcastic, or pessimistic when speaking with her. Depending on the situation, it may take her some time to get to the point where she does feel hope, God's love, and His promises. Basically, it takes as long as it takes. The supporting and healing process should never be rushed. You may see the solution long before she does, but she needs to come to that conclusion and resolution. When we communicate through humility, gentleness, patience, and unity, we are showing the example of Christ to our sisters, and these examples are where effective communication begins.

Importance of Effective Communication in Supporting Sisters

Now that we have established what effective communication is, let us notice its importance when supporting sisters. The support process centers around conversations. Carefully chosen words conveyed to the sister who needs support will lay the foundation for important conversations to begin. If words that are chosen initially do not offer support, hope, and godly resolutions, the support could be at risk. It is important to demonstrate to the sister that Christ will offer the solutions she needs to ease her struggles.

We note the guidance of Paul to Titus on the importance of choosing words wisely and controlling the tongue in Titus 2:3. We know this is important in every conversation we have with one another, but it is particularly important when supporting sisters. Words matter as they can have a profound influence and can be impactful to others. Remember, to communicate effectively, we must engage in active listening (see Chapter 5). Using active listening skills will aid you when choosing how to appropriately respond to her.

Wisdom Regarding Effective Communication from Proverbs

We have all been in situations where you said something, and immediately, when the words came out of your mouth, you wished you could just put them right back in. Or we have chosen words "off the cuff" to say at an inappropriate time. Scripture, especially the book of Proverbs, offers wisdom on how important effective communication is, especially when helping those who are hurting. We see a pattern of not only what to say but, just as importantly, when to speak words that will aid in supporting sisters. Consider the following passages:

- Proverbs 16:21: "The wise of heart is called discerning, and sweetness of speech increases persuasiveness." Always choose words that will be received as you intended. When sisters are in pain, it is not the time to offer, "I knew this would happen" or "I told you so." Emotions are usually heightened when a sister is coming to you for support, so choose words that will enable the most open lines of communication possible.

- Proverbs 16:24: "Gracious words are like a honeycomb, sweetness to the soul and health to the body." When we use gracious words, either in prayer or encouragement when supporting a sister, they will have a healing and encouraging effect. These words will be comforting, and she can keep close to her heart in challenging times.

- Proverbs 12:18: "There is one whose rash words are like sword thrusts, but the tongue of the wise brings healing." When supporting sisters, it is always important to use communication that gives clarity, helps to bring the focus to God's blessings and promises, and offers hope for the future.

- Proverbs 25:20: "Whoever sings songs to a heavy heart is like one who takes off a garment on a cold day, and like vinegar on soda." You never want to minimize a sister's pain or say things that could be construed as flippant and uncaring. Just as taking your coat off on a chilly day or adding vinegar to a wound, unempathetic words do not help sisters who are struggling.

- Proverbs 18:2: "A fool takes no pleasure in understanding, but only in expressing his opinion." Effective communication when supporting a sister in need is about listening and responding to her in a way that will be helpful. Simply put, it is not about you and what you believe. Always guide her to God's word and focus on finding the solutions there.

Practical Ways of Effective Communication

When supporting sisters in need, we want to use the most effective communication skills possible. The more you support your sisters, the more you will have the opportunity to sharpen your communication skills. Consider incorporating and practicing the following ways of effective communication:

- Think Before You Speak: By organizing your thoughts in advance, you can eliminate many of the awkward pauses that occur when speaking. It will also help you relay your information more concisely. While writing down your thoughts is not always possible in impromptu discussions, it is still effective to take a minute to organize your thoughts in your mind before you begin to speak. A good rule of thumb is to say, "This is what I am hearing you say," and repeat back the gist of what you are hearing and see if that is really what is being said. Oftentimes, when we repeat what was just said, the sister may realize that is not what she wanted to communicate. This method can also give her clarity on what she wants to convey.
- Be Clear and Concise with Your Vocabulary: The key to effective communication, especially when supporting a sister who is struggling, is to keep it simple with the words you choose. Be direct but loving and patient. The adage, "Mean what you say and say what you mean," applies here. When supporting a sister in need is not the time to use complex and convoluted communication. Notice the language she is using and use words that she will understand. You may have a brief time to make

a real impact, and you do not want unnecessary
vocabulary to get in the way. Always choose words
that are edifying (Ephesians 4:29), which will give
the sister you are supporting hope for the future
and help her understand solutions from God's
perspective.

As we support her, we want to seek to understand her
uniqueness and her struggles. Through our vocabulary, we
want her to understand that we are to be "imitators of God," as
we see in Ephesians 5:1.

- Speak with Confidence: Speaking in a confident
  manner will help you build trust with those you
  support. This confidence will come from knowing
  that God is blessing you and your ability to support
  sisters who are struggling. Confidence will also
  come from your knowledge of the Word. Always
  make sure that you do not become so busy with the
  support process that you neglect Bible study. If you
  are unsure how to best support a sister, always seek
  guidance from someone who does. This will also
  enable you to speak with confidence in knowing
  you are giving her the kind of support she needs.
- Be an Active Listener: See Chapter 5 for a
  complete discussion on active listening, but
  remember to "lean in" during the conversation,
  maintain eye contact, limit distractions, notice body
  language, and watch for nonverbal cues.
- Speak Truth in Love: An important part of
  supporting sisters who are struggling is to always
  show them love while speaking truth. Paul reminds
  us of this in his letter to the Ephesians. "Rather,

speaking the truth in love, we are to grow up in every way into him who is the head, into Christ (Ephesians 4:15)." As Christians, we know the most important part of any relationship is always standing firm in the truth of God's love and His promises. Many times, sharing truth with someone who is struggling may be difficult. They may not be emotionally ready to hear about God's love. But we can share truth in a way that is Christ-like and supportive.

- Remember Your Overall Purpose: In everything we do in support of our sisters, we want to bring glory to God. This includes the way we communicate with each other in a manner that is pleasing to Him (1 Corinthians 10:31).

Effective Communication Matters

In 1850, Charles Dickens visited the Telegraph Office at the Railway Station in Tonbridge, Kent, England. Although Dickens marveled at the speed of the electric telegraph and after witnessing the communication device, he is often attributed as commenting, "Electric communication will never be a substitute for the face of someone who with their soul encourages another person to be brave and true."[3] Although Dickens is associated with this quote from almost two centuries ago, it still applies today. In our modern world, effective communication is more important than ever. With the modern conveniences of social media, email, and smartphones, we have several ways to communicate with one another without meeting face-to-face. But when supporting sisters, the most effective way to communicate is face-to-face. Having a personal touch with someone who is hurting will make an impact on them. We see throughout scripture that Jesus was present and was near those He was ministering to.

When we support sisters who are struggling, words matter. The tone of those words matters. Our body language matters. We do not want emotions to guide the way we engage in conversation. We want God's Word to guide us in our effective communication with sisters who are struggling. It is a great responsibility to offer comfort to someone in need, and we want to make sure we are doing it in a godly manner, according to His teachings, and according to His will.

Questions for Discussion

1. When you engage in a conversation with someone, are you patient, or do you try to "hurry them up?" Do you believe being impatient is a habit, or is there something else going on?

2. Do you believe it is hard for Christians to speak truth in love? Why or why not? What are effective ways we can speak truth in love?

3. What are some practices that we can use to make sure we are choosing the right vocabulary when supporting sisters?

Chapter 9

Effective Communication, Part 2

The Importance of Asking the Right Kinds of Questions

The wise man doesn't give the right answers, he poses the right questions.

— *Claude Levi-Strauss*

Illumination

EVERY DAY in our lives we ask several types of questions. You may ask your husband, "What do you want for dinner?" You may ask an elderly neighbor, "I'm going to the store, is there anything you need?" You may ask your family, "Where should we go on summer vacation this year?" All these questions will elicit different types of responses. They may range from a simple "yes" or "no" response to more thought-provoking responses that have taken time to formulate an answer. The types of questions we want to ask when supporting sisters are questions that will make them pause and think about their responses. You want to guide them to consider different resolutions to determine how best to manage their struggles and what solutions align with God's law. As we continue the theme of building a house, one purpose of outside lighting on a house is to illuminate the property. Usually, outside lighting casts a larger range of light than lights you would find on the inside of the house. Asking the right kinds of questions to someone you are supporting functions like illumination. The right kinds of questions allow you to gain a more complete picture of the circumstances at hand and a wider perspective so you can examine and determine the kind of support that is needed.

Jesus, the Master Questioner

One of the most effective methods of teaching that Jesus used was asking questions. Throughout His ministry, He asked different types of questions as He taught to make His point and to get people to think. Let us notice just a few examples of questions He asked:

- In Matthew 5:13, He asked a question that could be easily answered: "You are the salt of the earth, but if salt has lost its taste, how shall its saltiness be restored?"
- In Luke 18:19, He asked a question that had no obvious answers: "And Jesus said to him, "Why do you call me good? No one is good except God alone."
- In Luke 7:42, He asked a question that He used to make a point: "When they could not pay, he cancelled the debt of both. Now which of them will love him more?"
- In Mark 12:14–15, He asked a question that made people think: And they came and said to him, "Teacher, we know that you are true and do not

care about anyone's opinion. For you are not
swayed by appearances, but truly teach the way of
God. Is it lawful to pay taxes to Caesar, or not?
Should we pay them, or should we not?" But,
knowing their hypocrisy, he said to them, "Why
put me to the test? Bring me a denarius and let me
look at it."

Jesus used questions to get people thinking and talking.
When we are supporting sisters, we want to do the same thing.
We want to understand their perspectives by engaging them in
the questions that give us information. We also want to ask
questions in a way that will give us clarity as to what their
struggles really are.

He Asked to Gain Information

Jesus was interested in engaging with others in a way to
understand their perspective. He did this through open-ended
questions that would allow them to think about their answer.
These questions often led to important conversations. We see
examples of this as He had a conversation on the road to
Emmaus and with a blind beggar. Notice how He asked questions to understand the perspectives of others and how He
guided them to understand their specific struggles. In Luke
24:17–20, after resurrecting from the dead, Jesus approached
two men walking along the road to Emmaus.

And he said to them, "What is this conversation that you are
holding with each other as you walk?"And they stood still,
looking sad. Then one of them, named Cleopas, answered
him, "Are you the only visitor to Jerusalem who does not
know the things that have happened there in these days?"

And he said to them, "What things?"And they said to him, "Concerning Jesus of Nazareth, a man who was a prophet mighty in deed and word before God and all the people, and how our chief priests and rulers delivered him up to be condemned to death and crucified him."

In this account, we see Jesus was concerned with the conversation that was taking place, and He wanted to know more about what was being said. After Cleopas asked Him a question, Jesus did not respond with an answer, but rather an open-ended question: what things? He knew this type of question would get the men talking, and He would have information about their concerns. Open-ended questions often bring clarity to a given situation.

In Mark 10, we read of the account of the blind beggar, Bartimaeus. Bartimaeus heard Jesus and shouted out for mercy. In Mark 10:51, Jesus asked him, "What do you want me to do for you?" In the account, Bartimaeus knew exactly who Jesus was, and the question that Jesus asked him could have had a host of answers. The question was asked in a way that Bartimaeus had to determine what was the most important thing that he needed Jesus to do for him. Bartimaeus answered that he wanted to see, and Jesus healed him because he had faith. Jesus asked an open-ended question to Bartimaeus, and his desire became known that he wanted to have his sight restored.

Jesus knew how to ask informative questions that allowed Him to find out what was important to people. If you want to be a good listener, learn to ask what, why, when, where, and how type questions that allow people to explain things from their own level of understanding. Open-ended questions will lead to a conversation and Lord willing, which will lead to healing! Although we discussed earlier the importance of active listening in Chapter 5, it is important to connect the role active listening plays to asking questions.

The Role Active Listening Plays in Questioning

When we first begin to support a sister who is struggling, it is important to listen and determine what her struggle is before we begin asking questions. We want this process not to be limited or rushed; we want her to tell her story as she sees fit. Listening to certain keywords that could help you determine her perspective will enable you to understand where her struggle stems from. Paul David Tripp, in his book *Instruments in the Redeemer's Hands: People in Need of Change Helping People in Need of Change*, notes the importance of letting the person tell their story. He refers to this as the "entry gate," stating, "The entry gate is not what you think the person is struggling with; it is the struggle the person confesses."[1] Active Listening is the basis of effective communication. It allows the struggling sister to explore her thoughts and feelings. She may then reach a different conclusion based on how a question is asked. This may cause her mindset to shift to reach a new solution. Active listening begins with asking good questions. The book of Proverbs highlights the importance of asking perceptive questions and seeking to understand:

- "A fool takes no pleasure in understanding, but only in expressing his opinion" (Proverbs 18:2).
- "If one gives an answer before he hears, it is his folly and shame" (Proverbs 18:13).
- "The purpose in a man's heart is like deep water, but a man of understanding will draw it out" (Proverbs 20:5).

We want to remember the wisdom from Proverbs and seek to understand the sister we are supporting. We can accomplish this by actively listening and asking questions that will give us the most information possible.

What Are Open-Ended Questions?

There are two types of questions that most people ask. They are closed-ended questions and open-ended questions. Closed-ended questions will provide a simple one- or two-word answer from the person you are asking. For example,

Q: "How was your day?"

A: "Good." OR

Q: "What is your favorite flavor of ice cream?"

A: "Chocolate."

Closed questions are useful when you are trying to gain simple information. We all use them every day in our conversations with others. But when we are supporting sisters who are struggling, we want to gain as much information as we can from them to determine how best to help them. We want to ask open-ended questions. Consider the following example of an open-ended question:

Q: "What is your favorite flavor of ice cream and why?"

A. "My favorite flavor is chocolate because every Friday night when I was younger, after dinner, my family would all go together and get ice cream, and that was a happy memory I have from my childhood!"

See the difference? You will usually learn more information if you ask open-ended questions.

How Will Asking Open-Ended Questions Help in Supporting Sisters?

It is all about conversation. We want the sister to begin and engage in conversation so we can determine how best to support her. Asking her open-ended questions can lead to:

- Thoughtful and Authentic Answers: Open-ended questions require someone to use critical thinking skills to provide an answer. The sister will need to think about how to respond to an answer because the question will not be answered with one or two words. Because she had carefully thought about her answers, greater insights and vulnerability will be uncovered.
- Improved Communication: Because open-ended questions lead to conversations, your active listening and communication skills will be used and will continue to be developed.
- Increased Confidence: Sisters who are struggling need to feel confident in seeking support and expressing themselves in a way that will help them clarify their perspectives and needs. Open-ended questions will allow for answers that will encourage her to continue to seek a godly resolution.

Open-ended questions will allow you to gain valuable information and insight. Open questions will begin with what, why, when, where, and how. Open questions will allow the respondent to be authentic in her answers and encourage her to analyze and think critically. Open questions will also allow you to respond with specific questions that will help to clarify her answers. Gary Collins, in his book *How to Be a People Helper*, discusses the importance of clarifying answers from the person you are supporting. He emphasizes the importance of trying to find out what has been done in the past to solve the problem. "Be aware of what the helpee is feeling, but try to find out, too, what he or she thinks now about the problem and what behavior may be contributing to the problem."[2] We always want to support the sister in a way that she can fully understand what her struggle is before she begins finding a solution.

Starting a Conversation Using Open-Ended Questions

Ask About Her Physical Wellbeing

Ask questions that will help her identify physical issues such as problems with sleep, a healthy diet, exercise, water intake, etc. Many times, when sisters are struggling, they do not think about taking care of their physical bodies, and this plays a role in how they are coping emotionally. If she is not taking care of her body, real emotions (or perceived) struggles will be heightened.

Ask Gentle Questions that Identify Perspectives

Ask gentle questions that will get her to start thinking. Such as "What are some issues that you need to consider?" or "What would a positive outcome look like to you?" By asking "what" types of questions, you are allowing her time to consider her answer without being influenced as to how you think about the situation. "What" types of questions will encourage thought-provoking answers, help clarify the struggle, and help you identify her perspective.

Understanding the Difference between Emotions and Feelings

According to *Psychology Today,*

> Emotions originate as sensations in the body. Feelings are influenced by our emotions but are generated from our mental thoughts. Emotions are the raw data, a reaction to the present reality, whereas feelings can be diluted by stories we've created in our head based on events of the past or fears of the future—not necessarily the truth of the situation.[3]

Emotions and feelings are not the same, but we often use the words interchangeably. Emotions can be powerful. God gave us emotions to help protect us from dangerous situations, to help us with communication, to motivate us, and to help us understand each other. But emotions can lead to feelings that often are not reality. Feelings can change very quickly. For the sister who is struggling, it is important for her to identify emotions and feelings that follow for what they are. Asking open-ended questions, such as "What was going on in your physical environment when you first felt this way?" triggers such as smell, sight, hearing, etc., can cause you to remember something that may not be pleasant. Encouraging the sister to become aware of what is going on around her could be helpful.

Encouraging a Path Forward

For the sister who is struggling, many times, she can only see the present. At an appropriate time, encourage her to start thinking about the future. Questions like "What do you want a year from now to look like?" or "How are you going to make _____ happen?" You may want to engage in goal setting to help identify a plan forward. Sisters who are struggling usually feel stuck and cannot see past tomorrow.

It is helpful to encourage them to understand that part of healing is to look to the future and to particularly see how they can serve God and others for His glory.

Open-Ended Questions to Consider

The following are examples of Open-Ended Questions that you might like to ask that will get the conversation started.

- What caused you to reach out to me?
- What does a typical day look like for you, and how does that make you feel?
- In what ways is your struggle impacting your thought process? In your spiritual life? In your relationships?
- How do you manage your stress, and what strategies work for you?
- How would you describe your overall well-being?

Because Jesus is Lord, He always knew the right kinds of questions to ask given the situation. He was aware of the circumstances of those He spoke with and the issues that were at hand. This allowed Him to ask the right kinds of questions that would allow them to think about a solution. When we are supporting sisters who are in need, it is not our responsibility to give them the answers to their struggles. It is our responsibility to guide them in their thinking so they will come to a godly resolution. The right kinds of questions will do just that. Active listening and asking the right questions are the most powerful ways to ensure effective communication when supporting sisters.

Questions for Discussion

1. When supporting sisters, how can understanding her perspective help us to determine the right kinds of questions to ask? What are some beneficial ways to understand her perspective?
2. Study deeper into the types of questions that Jesus asked. How can we model the types of questions He asked when we are supporting sisters?
3. Compile a list of open-ended questions that might be helpful to ask when you are supporting sisters.

Chapter 10

Tool 6: How to Maintain a Patient and Calm Demeanor

A patient man has great understanding, but a quick-tempered man displays folly.

— *Proverbs* 14:29

Insulation as Stability

MAINTAINING a patient and calm demeanor during stressful situations can be a struggle for some of us. Depending on the circumstance, being patient and calm might be nearly impossible. Proverbs 17:27 tells us that "Whoever restrains his words has knowledge, and he who has a cool spirit is a man of understanding." Matthew Henry comments referring to cool spirit, "He is of a cool spirit (so some read it), not heated with passion, nor put into any tumult or disorder by the impetus of any corrupt affection, but even and stayed. A cool head with a warm heart is an admirable composition."[1] This will indicate wisdom as a person will stay calm under pressure and not be moved by heightened emotions and circumstances.

We know of several professions where a patient and calm demeanor is a must: emergency room personnel, surgeons, teachers, first responders, and customer service representatives, just to name a few. When supporting sisters who are struggling, we also must maintain a patient and calm demeanor. Hopefully, this will begin the supporting relationship on a positive note.

We can compare having a patient and calm demeanor when supporting sisters to the insulation in a house. Insulation is needed in a house to keep the desired temperature inside the house year-round. Insulation keeps the house warm in the winter and cool in the summer. Keeping a patient and calm demeanor when supporting sisters is like insulation. Just as insulation keeps the temperature of the house even, not too hot or too cold, maintaining a patient and calm demeanor will keep the support relationship moving forward. This chapter will focus on the examples we see from scripture of the importance of maintaining a patient and calm demeanor and practical ways where we can focus when supporting sisters in need.

Examples of Maintaining a Patient and Calm Demeanor in Scripture

Throughout scripture, there are accounts of those who demonstrated maintaining a calm demeanor in difficult circumstances. Although such circumstances vary within the accounts, we read of several times when Jesus Himself had to remain patient and calm in difficult times. He faced unusual situations, different personalities, and several who tested his patience. We also see a pattern of others who maintained a patient and calm demeanor during trying times. Consider the following:

- In Luke 4, we read of the Temptation of Jesus by the devil. Jesus had been in the wilderness and had nothing to eat for forty days. Scripture tells us that He was hungry. The devil came to tempt and mock Him. Even though Jesus was hungry, tempted, and mocked, He remained calm as He responded to the devil.
- In Luke 8, we read about a storm that caused angst among the disciples. They were in a boat when the wind picked up, and the boat began to fill with water. Jesus was asleep during the storm. He remained calm as the storm ceased.
- In John 19, Jesus responded calmly to Pilate after being asked about the authority that Pilate had.
- Esther, realizing that she had to save her people, was calm when she talked to the King about Haman's plot to kill the Jews. She remained calm when she went before the King, explained the situation, and successfully saved her people.
- In 1 Samuel 25, we read of the account of David and Abigail. Abigail took matters into her own hands and spoke calmly to David, hoping he would not harm her husband, Nabal.
- In everything that Job endured, he remained calm as he did not curse God as his wife had suggested.

We see a pattern throughout Scripture of the importance of maintaining a patient and calm demeanor in difficult circumstances. This is no different when supporting sisters who are in need.

The Importance of a Patient and Calm Demeanor

Maintaining a patient and calm demeanor when supporting sisters will be helpful for a variety of reasons, including:

- Supports Appropriate Reaction: When supporting a sister, we always want to keep a level head and be proactive instead of reactive. When supporting someone who is struggling, emotions can run high, so we want to be calm and patient. I always think about children when they fall and skin a knee. The first thing they do is look at the adult to see their reaction. If the adult reacts with a gasp and begins running for the Band-Aids, the child will usually burst into tears. But if the adult calmly reacts, helps the child up, brushes the knee off, the child usually does not go into hysterics. The child will react accordingly based on how the adult reacts. Now, I am not comparing a sister who is struggling with difficult issues to a child with a skinned knee, but I do believe the sister in need will look and see what our reaction will be. In my experience, it is always best to show empathy and be compassionate, but to not let your chin drop to the floor in reaction to something that was just said!

- Creates a Safe Space: Demonstrating a patient and calm demeanor will create a safe space for the sister who is struggling. Because of the calm environment that you have created, she will feel at ease knowing personal struggles will be confidential and she will not be judged.

- Creates an Environment of Trust: Being patient and calm will create an environment of trust because you, as the supporter, are engaging in active listening and effective communication skills. Because of your demeanor, you can listen, ask appropriate questions, and respond in a clear, concise manner.

We have established that demonstrating a patient and calm demeanor is needed when supporting sisters. But this can be difficult at times to maintain. Let us note ways that will enable us to demonstrate a patient and calm demeanor.

Practical Ways to Maintain a Patient and Calm Demeanor

- Take Care of Yourself: Make sure you are getting enough sleep, eating a healthy diet, exercising, engaging in self-care, and staying in God's word. Supporting others can be physically exhausting. When your mind, body, and soul are at peace, you will demonstrate patience and calmness.
- Practice Mindfulness Techniques: Mindfulness techniques such as deep breathing, journaling, taking a nature walk, or meditating on scripture will help keep you calm.
- Set Healthy Boundaries: Keep your priorities in mind so you do not become overwhelmed.
- Reflect on Your Emotions: Be self-aware of your emotions and feelings and recognize your personal triggers to certain situations.

- Model Patience and Calmness: If the sister you are supporting is anxious, you should model a calm voice, a relaxed posture, a relaxed look on your face, and a patient demeanor with her.
- Start Easy: She may be anxious talking to you at first. Reassure her that she is in a safe environment with no judgment. Talk about trivial things at the beginning if she is anxious to make her comfortable, such as cooking, sewing, gardening, sports, etc.
- Pray: Beginning your conversation with a prayer will always calm the situation for both of you. We will discuss more about prayer in Chapter 13.

Think back to a time when you encountered a stressful situation. Maybe you had a difficult conversation with someone, or something happened where emotions were heightened. Think about how you responded to those situations. Were you proactive or reactive? Did you demonstrate a patient and calm demeanor, or were you frantic? When situations are stressful, it can be quite easy to "lose your cool," but that usually never helps the situation. When we are aware of the importance of remaining patient and calm, that awareness will help us when we support sisters who are in need.

We discussed earlier the importance of insulation in a house. Insulation in a house functions as a protector that prevents the transmission of heat or cold. A patient and calm demeanor will function as a protector when supporting sisters. When you support sisters, emotions can become out of control. Your patient and calm demeanor will function as the stabilizer or insulation against emotional and/or irrational feelings. We always want to remember James 3:17, "But the wisdom from above is first pure, then peaceable, gentle, open to reason, full of mercy and good fruits, impartial and sincere," and do all we can to demonstrate a calm and patient demeanor when supporting sisters!

Questions for Discussion

1. Reflect on a time when you experienced a patient and calm demeanor during a stressful situation. How did your demeanor help to ease tensions?
2. What methods can we learn from those in scripture who maintained a patient and calm demeanor?
3. Discuss the importance of creating a safe space in relation to maintaining a patient and calm demeanor.

Chapter 11

Tool 7: Made in the Image of God

So, God created man in his own image, in the image of God he created him; male and female he created him.

— Genesis 1:27

Portraying Good Landscaping

WHEN GOD CREATED THE WORLD, He did so in a logical, ordered manner. We see in Genesis 1 that everything He created was good. God created man in His own image (Genesis 1:27–28, 5:1, 9:6; Romans 8:29; 1 Corinthians 11:7; 2 Corinthians 3:18; Ephesians 4:24; Colossians 3:10; James 3:9). He created man for several reasons including to reflect the nature of God and who He is, to have a relationship with God, and to bring others to Him. Before sin entered the world, Adam and Eve were the perfect examples of God's image. They lived in complete harmony with nature and were naked and not ashamed. God had created the world and every living creature, and it was good. Now, we know the rest of the story of how sin came about, and we as Christians must work every day to live up to the image of God. We all possess this image to some degree, but not perfectly.

Because we, as Christians, are His representatives on Earth, we carry a great responsibility. We have the ability to think and reason, and we have souls. But we also have free will, and we have a choice to be obedient and do God's will or not (Deuteronomy 30:19, Matthew 22:37, John 3:14–21). This responsibility should not be taken lightly, and everything we do must be for His glory. Being made in God's image can be compared to a landscaped yard. Portraying good landscaping around a house represents the owner's desire to maintain a nice, well-maintained yard. It is important for us to believe we are made in His image and realize it is our whole self, not just parts of our self. Once we have this belief, what we care about and how we care about things will change. As Christians, we want to portray our whole self in the image of God correctly as we offer support to sisters who are struggling.

What Type of Image Do You Project?

Before we support sisters, we need to make sure we are projecting the correct image of God in our lives. Engage in self-reflection and consider the following:

- Do you live your life in a manner pleasing to God? Do you live a life of order or chaos?
- Do you encourage others by your words, actions, or deeds? Are you willing to help those in need?
- Do you offer hope to those who are suffering?
- Do you have a godly attitude of service?

- Are you obedient to God's will, and is that reflected in your everyday life?
- Do you find yourself saying, "I don't want to get involved," or "She did this to herself because of the decisions she made," or "I have nothing to offer her?"

Sometimes, we need to stop and evaluate our own lives and make sure we are living in accordance with the image of God. When traveling on an airplane, the first thing they tell you in case of an emergency is to put your oxygen mask on first before you begin to help others. God is our oxygen mask, and if we are not living a life obedient to Him, we will not be effective in supporting sisters who are in need. How do we, as supporters, reflect the image of God? For our purposes in trying to reflect the image of God to our sisters who are struggling, I want to focus on the image of God as helper, comforter, counselor.

As a Helper

When you hear the description of helper, what comes to your mind? A helper usually does not get recognition that the person who is in charge does. They may be treated less than by society. They are supporters; they work quietly behind the scenes. Remember, God made Eve as a "helpmeet" to Adam (Genesis 2:18). She was to function as a complement to Adam. We see in Exodus 18:4 that one of Moses's sons was named Eliezer, which means "God of Help," referring to the way God had helped lead the children of Israel away from Pharaoh's sword.[1] We also see God as our help and shield (Psalm 33:20). From a biblical perspective, a helper is a characteristic of Jesus. We see many examples throughout scripture of various ways Jesus helped. Notice the following:

- He served others: Jesus described Himself as a servant, saying, "The Son of Man did not come to be served, but to serve" (Mark 10:45). He lived as a servant by obeying God's will and washing the feet of His disciples (John 13:1–20).
- He helps those who sin: "My little children, I am writing these things to you so that you may not sin. But if anyone does sin, we have an advocate with the Father, Jesus Christ the righteous" (1 John 2:1).
- He sent the Spirit of Truth (Holy Spirit): "And I will ask the Father, and he will give you another Helper, to be with you forever, even the Spirit of truth, whom the world cannot receive, because it neither sees him nor knows him. You know him, for he dwells with you and will be in you" (John 14:16–17).
- He helps those through healing: One example of His helping through healing is the woman with the issue of blood in Mark 5:25–29.

As a Comforter

Jesus offered comfort to many people He encountered. When Lazarus died, He was there to comfort Mary and Martha by assuring them Lazarus would rise again (John 11:23). Before He left to be crucified, He comforted his disciples by promising He would prepare a place for them, and the Holy Spirit would be with them and guide them (John 14).

Jesus offers us comfort in many ways. For example, when we are suffering He is the God of all comfort (2 Corinthians 1:3–5), He will provide a way of escape when we are tempted (1 Corinthians 10:13), when we are anxious, we can cast all of our cares on Him because He cares for us (1 Peter 5:7), and if we are faithful to Him, He will never leave us or forsake us (Deuteronomy 31:8). We have comfort that if we are obedient to Him and do His will, we will have a home with Him in heaven. That is the greatest comfort! We can learn from His example of comfort and do our best to reflect that to our sisters who are struggling.

As a Counselor

In Isaiah 9:6, we see where Jesus is referred to as counselor, "For to us a child is born, to us a son is given; and the government shall be upon his shoulder, and his name shall be called Wonderful Counselor, Mighty God, Everlasting Father, Prince of Peace." The title "Wonderful Counselor" brings to mind someone who has wisdom and can offer guidance. We know this to be true as this prophecy from Isaiah was eventually fulfilled. As Christians, we know that His counsel is the most valuable as we navigate life on this earth. "He is the only Counselor who ever had 'the words of eternal life' (John 6:68), His counsel alone is truthfully described as 'the light of the world,' and His counsel only will judge men at the last day (John 12:48)."[2] When we think of the best ways to support women who are struggling, we want to make sure that we always keep in mind that we are created in God's image. The three images of Christ as helper, comforter, and counselor embody the very characteristics we have discussed in previous chapters. In some form or fashion, all of these three images have their foundations based on love, compassion, and empathy. We should replicate, to the best of our ability, the characteristics of helper, comforter, and counselor when supporting women in need.

In his book, *Jesus the Greatest Therapist Who Ever Lived*,

Mark Baker discusses the fact that we are relational people. We were created to walk alongside others in joy and in sorrow. We have an example of the relationship between the Father, Son, and Holy Spirit, as seen in John 1:1. And because of this, "our capacity for relationship reflects the image of God on earth."[3] When sisters struggle, it always affects their relationships with others—friends, family, acquaintances, or their relationship with God to some degree. Even if they are dealing with internal struggles such as stress, anxiety, loneliness, etc., it still affects relationships with others and, most likely, with God. We want to offer support, hope, and love so their relationships can be healthy and reflect the image of God.

As Christians who try every day to live up to the image of God, we are all broken, and we all sin and fall short of the glory of God. But through Jesus, we have been given grace and mercy to continue every day to do His will. When we support sisters who are struggling, we must always follow God's word and not waiver because we might hurt someone's feelings. We can speak the truth in a kind and loving way, but we must always speak the truth. Sisters have issues that are sometimes complex and will take time to work through. We have the inspired Word to guide us. As we continue to do His will, He has equipped all of us with special qualities that will allow us to be His best representatives on earth while we are supporting our sisters in need. What a blessing He has given us as sisters in Christ!

Questions for Discussion

1. What does being made in God's image mean to you? What responsibility, if any, do you feel, and how does that affect the way you live your life?

2. In what ways are you a helper, a comforter, and a counselor to sisters? How can you improve these areas?

3. Self-reflect on the questions found within the section, "What Type of Image Do You Project?" Do you feel comfortable?

Chapter 12

Tool 8: How to Know When to Refer

Bringing in Professionals

Without counsel plans fail, but with many advisers they succeed.

— *Proverbs 15:22*

THIS BOOK HAS PROVIDED you with basic counseling tools that can be used when you are supporting sisters who are struggling. These tools can be applied to situations that might be tenuous, stressful, and emotional. But it is important to know when to bring in someone who has had professional training in the mental health field, should it be necessary. As we continue our theme of building a house, as you begin to build, unless you are an expert in building a house, you will more than likely seek those individuals who are experts in construction. It would be foolish and dangerous for you to have someone build your house that does not have the knowledge or expertise in construction. This same line of thinking can be applied to making sure you know when to seek out guidance from the mental health community.

I am not a licensed professional counselor. I am a biblical counselor who has been trained to offer counsel based on God's law and guidance. With this training comes responsibility to know how far my training will allow me to counsel sisters. Above all, I have been trained to do no harm. There have been many times when I have had to tell a sister that I can be part of her support team, but I would like to refer her to a trusted mental health professional because I am not equipped or trained for her specific issue. I have told her I would make phone calls on her behalf and even offer to accompany her to the appointment if she wishes. However, I made it clear to her that my training in biblical counseling would only allow me to do so much.

As helpers who are compassionate, caring, and empathetic, we want to make sure we provide the best counsel for our sisters. As you continue to support another, you may become aware of issues where a mental health professional needs to be consulted. You may have a "gut feeling" or become uncomfortable with your support and that is perfectly fine. It does not mean you have failed your sister. Remember, we want to find the way to best help the sister. Gary Collins, in his book *Christian Counseling: A Comprehensive Guide* suggests, "A referral is an acknowledgement that no one person has the time, stamina, emotional stability, knowledge, skill or experience to help everyone." [1] If a referral is needed, it is important to convey to her the importance of building a support team around her and you can be part of her team.

Biblical Examples of Those Who Asked for Help and Had Specific Areas of Expertise

During Bible times, much like today, we see examples of how

people with unique skills or expertise were helpful. Observe the following:

- General Occupations: Throughout the Bible, we have descriptions of people who held certain occupations that required specific skills. For example: baker (Genesis 40:1), butler or cupbearer (Nehemiah 1:11), cooks (1 Samuel 9:23–24), fishermen (Isaiah 19:8; Matthew 4:18), hunter (Jeremiah 16:16), shepherds (Luke 2:8), farmers (Genesis 4:2), scribes (Ezra 7:6), carpenter (2 Samuel 5:11), coppersmith (2 Timothy 4:14), goldsmith (Nehemiah 3:8), silversmith (Acts 19:24), tentmaking (Acts 18:3), just to name a few. All of these occupations and specialized skills were needed during Bible times, and the general population relied on these individuals.

- Bezalel and Oholiab: These two men may not be familiar to you, but they were instrumental in carrying out a specific task for God. We read of God revealing to Moses the plan for the design and building of the Tabernacle. "I have filled him with the Spirit of God, with ability and intelligence, with knowledge and all craftsmanship, to devise artistic designs, to work in gold, silver, and bronze, in cutting stones for setting, and in carving wood, to work in every craft" (Exodus 31:3–5). God gave these two craftsmen the skills and ability to work with their hands, and He used them in an important way. This is a reminder for us to always be ready and willing to use the talents that God has given us to serve others.

- Daniel: God gave Daniel the ability to interpret dreams. We read of this ability in Daniel 2 and his interpretation of a dream by King Nebuchadnezzar. The King needed an explanation of a dream he had, so Daniel offered his skills. We know that the King was pleased with what Daniel told him and promoted Daniel as "ruler of Babylon" as noted in Daniel 2:48. However, Daniel remained in the King's court (Daniel 2:49).

Just like today, we all seek out professionals when we need a particular task, job, or consultation that needs to be completed. This is no different when we need to refer a sister to a mental health professional.

How to Know When to Refer

When supporting sisters in need, it is important to be aware of when the appropriate time is to refer them to a mental health professional. You will want to consider the following and encourage her to seek out a mental health professional when:

- Her symptoms seem to be severe, and she cannot manage them on her own.
- She is not progressing in the supporting relationship. Speaking with someone else might be helpful to her to learn to manage her struggles in a healthy manner.
- She has complex medical conditions. Many times, other medical conditions might contribute to mental health issues. This would be an appropriate time to seek out a mental health professional.

- You have concerns about her safety or the safety of others.
- You are beyond what you feel comfortable supporting. Remember, our goal is to do no harm and to support the sister the best way we can.

When you are supporting a sister in need, awareness will be key. You will want to be cognizant of her mindset, emotions, and behaviors in order to determine if a referral is warranted.

Practical Ways to Help Reinforce Your Counseling Tools

When you are supporting sisters who are struggling, it is important to have current information on mental health professionals when you need to make a referral. You want to look for Christian helpers who are established in the mental health community, for example, licensed professional counselors, social workers, psychologists, substance abuse counselors, marriage and family therapists, and psychiatrists. Talk to these professionals whom you trust and ask them to offer guidance on the next steps. Start by asking your church leadership who they recommend when they need to refer members. You can also ask members of the congregation if they have any experience with the mental health community and seek their recommendations. Usually, word of mouth, reputation, and the recommendation of others is an excellent starting place when compiling your list. You can also reach out to the brotherhood universities that have counseling programs to see if they have an alumni directory for someone in your area. After you have compiled your list, make sure it is kept current, and share it with your leadership at your congregation.

When you decide a referral is needed, patience and

speaking truth in love will go far. Let the sister know you are here for her, and you will still be supportive. Many people do not seek out professional counseling because of the stigma still associated with this type of support. Give her time to make that decision to seek further support because counseling will not be effective if she is not fully committed to additional support. Pray for her and with her that she will make the best decision given her struggles.

Questions for Discussion

1. Do you believe there is a stigma, especially for Christians, to reach out to the mental health community for help? Why or why not?
2. Discuss what it means to you to "do no harm."
3. In what ways can you help build an effective support team surrounding the sister in need?

Chapter 13

The Tool Above All Other Tools: Prayer

Likewise the Spirit helps us in our weakness. For we do not know what to pray for as we ought, but the Spirit himself intercedes for us with groanings too deep for words. And he who searches hearts knows what is the mind of the Spirit, because the Spirit intercedes for the saints according to the will of God.

— Romans 8:26–27

THROUGHOUT THIS BOOK, I have compared the tools that will help you support a sister in need to building a house. All of the tools that were described in previous chapters are important, but the most valuable tool we use is prayer. Just as prayer fills our homes during times of happiness and sadness, prayer is an integral part of supporting our sisters.

When sisters are struggling, either with personal sin, the sin of others that is causing them pain, or simply the stresses of living in a fallen world, the best comfort we can give them is prayer. As we experience the joys and the heartaches in life, we know the comfort and power of Christians offering prayer on behalf of others is vital (James 5:16). Prayer is woven into everything we do, especially when supporting others. We see an example of this in Mark 14: 32–34,

> And they went to a place called Gethsemane. And he said to his disciples, "Sit here while I pray." And he took with him Peter and James and John and began to be greatly distressed and troubled. And he said to them, "My soul is very sorrowful, even to death. Remain here and watch."

Even though Jesus knew what lay before Him, He reached out and asked those closest to Him to remain by His side. He prayed to the Father while the others simply sat beside Him as a source of comfort. We can offer our sisters who are struggling the same example.

Prayer is not just necessary for the sister who is struggling, it is also necessary for you as her supporter. Let us notice these two points of view and how we can incorporate prayer as we support sisters.

Prayer Perspective from You as the Helper

When you support a sister who is struggling, the responsibility is great. You have made yourself available to listen, support, encourage, and offer hope to a sister who may feel there is no hope. As Christians, we know that prayer is powerful. Prayer will help to bring comfort, lessen anxious feelings, and provide strength to you as the helper. Pray for guidance, wisdom, and strength to help you in the supporting relationship. Prayer also serves as a reminder that we are dependent on God. We are serving Him when we support our sisters who are in need. When we ask for wisdom, the Holy Spirit will guide our hearts and minds in the best way to support her through our words, thoughts, and deeds. Praying before you begin a conversation with a sister who is struggling will give you peace and clarity that only God can offer. Everything that is done in the supporting relationship is working to bring her closer to Christ and for her to make decisions that will allow His will to be done.

Prayer Perspective from the Sister in Need

James 5:13 tells us, "Is anyone among you suffering? Let him pray. Is anyone cheerful? Let him sing praise." As Christians, prayer is integral in everything we do. We always want to encourage those we support to take their struggles to the Father. However, when we are suffering, praying can become difficult. Many pray as a last resort to discover a resolution. As supporters of those who are struggling, we want to model the importance of prayer when dealing with concerns. We read in Matthew 6:5–13, where Jesus instructed his disciples to pray. Paul tells Timothy that he is constantly praying for him (2 Timothy 1:3). We want to encourage the sister to pray daily about her situation and also to have a place to pray where she is away from distractions. Prayer provides a source of hope and guidance for the sister who is in pain, and this will aid in her healing. If she is having trouble gaining clarity in her prayers, you might suggest that she write out her prayers. Many people find the acronym ACTS (Adoration, Confession, Thanksgiving, Supplication) helpful when knowing what to pray about. This will help her to focus on specific needs, concerns, and thanksgiving and also serve as a record of reflection when situations are resolved. This will give her comfort and enable her to see how God is working in her life (Romans 8:28).

Concluding Thoughts

When I look back over the tools I have presented to you, there are common themes that will help you to establish effective support for sisters in need. Before you can begin a supporting relationship, trust must be established. This will take time for a sister who is struggling to feel comfortable enough to talk to you about her deepest pain. Nurture the relationship and offer comfort and hope, and eventually, when she feels comfortable, she will open up to you. After trust has been established, hopefully, healing can begin. It is also important for a sister to know you are there for them. Many times, struggles can become so severe, and she needs to know you are there to offer her support. Sitting with her and not talking or offering to meet her for coffee might be the best thing you can do for her at that moment. We have discussed extensively the role active listening plays in the relationship. I believe this cannot be overstated. Taking the time to be attentive to her needs and listening to her pain will go a long way in the healing process.

Finally, empathy is a must. The most loving response you can give someone in pain is to put yourself in her shoes and understand her perspective. Sisters who are hurting want to be heard and understood, and you might be the only person in their life who can do that for them! As Christians, supporting one another is something that we do. When someone is sick, has a baby, or experiences a death in the family, we automatically bring food for support. We support the elderly, orphans, widows, and anyone else who has a need. Supporting a sister who is struggling with her mental health should be no different. We all need someone that we can confide in to discuss personal matters, and it is comforting to know that we have sisters who can offer support. Paul reminds us in Philippians 2:15 to be lights of the world. There is no better way to let our lights shine than to support one another during times of struggle. I pray this book will be used to equip you in ministering to others to build up the body of Christ (Ephesians 4:12), and this ministry is for His glory (1 Corinthians 10:31).

Questions for Discussion

1. Why do you think it is hard for some who are suffering to pray?

2. Have there been times in your life when you found it hard to pray? Discuss the circumstances and how you resolved this.

3. What are some ways you can support a sister in need if she does not want to talk?

4. In what ways has this study offered encouragement to you and/or equipped you to help sisters in need?

5. The devil will always be there to plant seeds of doubt in our abilities to support sisters. How can we quiet those doubts and focus on using the abilities that God has equipped us with to help each other?

Notes

Introduction: Christ as Cornerstone

1. Michael Gembola, "An Interview with Three Women in Counseling Ministry," *Journal of Biblical Counseling* 35 (2021): 89.
2. Gembola, "An Interview," 91.
3. Kim Chalmers, "Practicum: Support for Women: A Model for Teaching Biblical Counseling Tools," Florence, AL: Heritage Christian University, April 10, 2023.

1. Biblical Support of Counseling

1. https://www.merriam-webster.com/dictionary/counsel?utm_campaign=sd&utm_medium=serp&utm_source=jsonld.
2. Vine's Dictionary: Yâ'ats (יָעַץ, Strong's #3289), "those who give counsel."

2. Biblical Support of Women to Women Counseling

1. William Hendriksen, *New Testament Commentary: Exposition of the Pastoral Epistles* (Grand Rapids: Baker Book House, 1957), 365.
2. Elyse Fitzpatrick and Carol Cornish, eds., *Women Helping Women: A Biblical Guide to the Major Issues Women Face* (Eugene, OR: Harvest House Publishers, 1997), 61.

3. Developing the Right Mindset

1. https://www.pray.com/articles/what-is-selfawareness#:~:text=Self%2Dawareness%20is%20a%20form,is%20the%20beginning%20of%20wisdom.%E2%80%9D
2. To learn more about the importance of establishing boundaries, see Henry Cloud and John Townsend, *Boundaries: When to Say Yes and How to Say No to Take Control of Your Life* (Grand Rapids: Zondervan, 1992).

4. Tool 1: Demonstrating Compassion

1. https://www.dictionary.com/browse/compassion.
2. See www.Rosiesgarage.org for additional information.
3. Heather S. Lonczak, "20 Reasons Why Compassion Is So Important in Psychology," *Positive Psychology*, 7 June 2019. https://positivepsychology.com/why-is-compassion-important.

5. Tool 2: Active Listening

1. Linda Clark, *5 Leadership Essentials for Women: Developing Your Ability to Make Things Happen* (Birmingham: New Hope Publishers, 2004), 37.
2. *Communication in the Real World: An Introduction to Communication Studies*. Open Textbook Library. Minneapolis: University of Minnesota Libraries. 29 September 2016 doi:10.24926/8668.0401.
3. Dianna Booher, *The Esther Effect: The Seven Secrets of Self-Confidence and Influence* (Nashville: W. Publishing Group, 2001), 87-88.
4. Bill Bagents and Rosemary Snodgrass, *Counseling for Church Leaders: A Practical Guide* (Florence, AL: Heritage Christian University Press, 2021), 66-67.

6. Tool 3: Demonstrating Empathy

1. Jamil Zali, "Making Empathy Central to Your Company Culture," *Harvard Business Review*, https://hbr.org/2019/05/making-empathy-central-to-your-company-culture.
2. https://www.merriam-webster.com/dictionary/empathy.
3. https://cultureofempathy.com/References/Experts/Carl-Rogers-Quotes.htm.
4. For more information about Developmental Stages of Empathy see https://positivepsychology.com/empathy-worksheets/
5. Gary Collins, *Christian Counseling: A Comprehensive Guide*, 3rd ed. (Nashville: Thomas Nelson, 2007), 67.
6. Robert W. Gauger, "Toward an Example of Pastoral Care: Considering the Life of Jesus," *Journal of Pastoral Care and Counseling*, 68 (2014): 4–5.

7. Tool 4: Demonstrating a Christ-Like Love

1. For more information on Skin-to-Skin contact and its impact on human

development, see https://www.ncbi.nlm.nih.gov/pmc/articles/PMC533 0336/.

8. Tool 5: Effective Communication – Part 1

1. https://www.indeed.com/career-advice/career-development/how-to-improve-verbalcommunicationskills#:~:text=What%20are%20verbal%20communication%20skills,Using%20humor%20to%20engage%20audiences.
2. Paul David Tripp, *War of Words: Getting to the Heart of Our Communication Struggles* (Phillipsburg: P&R Publishing, 2000), 55.
3. For more information about Dickens' visit to Tonbridge, see https://www.tonbridgehistory.org.uk/events/dickens-telegraph.htm.

9. Effective Communication, Part 2

1. Paul David Tripp, *Instruments in the Redeemer's Hands: People in Need of Change Helping People in Need of Change* (Phillipsburg: P&R Publishing, 2002), 127.
2. Gary Collins, *How to Be a People Helper* (Carol Stream, IL: Tyndale Momentum, 1995), 64.
3. https://www.psychologytoday.com/intl/blog/the-pleasure-is-all-yours/202202/the-important-difference-between-emotions-and-feelings.

10. Tool 6: How to Maintain a Patient and Calm Demeanor

1. https://www.biblegateway.com/resources/matthew-henry/Proverbs 17.27.

11. Tool 7: Made in the Image of God

1. Strong's H461.
2. https://www.studylight.org/commentaries/eng/bcc/isaiah-9.html.
3. Mark W. Baker, *Jesus the Greatest Therapist Who Ever Lived* (New York: HarperOne, 2007), 52.

12. Tool 8: How to Know When to Refer

1. Gary R. Collins, *Christian Counseling: A Comprehensive Guide,* 3rd ed (Nashville: Thomas Nelson: 2007), 80.

Resource List

The following are recommended resources for you to help support sisters who are struggling. It is a mixture of brotherhood and secular authors. As with any book you read, "keep the fish and throw away the bones."

Bagents, Bill and Rosemary Snodgrass. *Counseling for Church Leaders: A Practical Guide*. Florence, AL: Heritage Christian University Press, 2021.

Baker, Mark W. *Jesus the Greatest Therapist Who Ever Lived*. New York: HarperOne, 2007.

Carter, Les. *Broken Vows: How to Put the Pieces of a Marriage Back Together*. Nashville: Thomas Nelson, 1991.

Cloud, Henry and John Townsend. *Safe People: How to Find Relationships That Are Good for You and Avoid Those That Aren't*. Grand Rapids: Zondervan, 1995.

———. *Boundaries With Kids: When to Say Yes, When to Say No to Help Your Children Gain Control of Their Lives*. Grand Rapids: Zondervan, 1998.

———. *Boundaries in Marriage*. Grand Rapids: Zondervan, 1999.

Collins, Gary R. *How to Be a People Helper*. Carol Stream, IL: Tyndale, 1995.

———. *Christian Counseling: A Comprehensive Guide*, 3rd ed., Nashville: Thomas Nelson, 2007.

Crabb, Lawrence J., Jr. *Effective Biblical Counseling: A Model for Helping Caring Christians Become Capable Counselors*. Grand Rapids: Ministry Resources Library, 1977.

Evans, Patricia. *The Verbally Abusive Relationship: How to Recognize It and How to Respond*. 2nd ed. Holbrook, MA: Adams Media, 1996.

Fitzpatrick, Elyse and Carol Cornish. *Women Helping Women: A Biblical Guide to the Major Issues Women Face*. Eugene, OR: Harvest House Publishers, 1997.

Flatt, Bill. *Building a Healthy Family*. Nashville: Gospel Advocate, 1993.

———. *Restoring My Soul: The Pursuit of Spiritual Resilience*. Nashville: Gospel Advocate, 2001.

Hislop, Bev. *Shepherding Women in Pain: Real Women, Real Issues, and What You Need to Know to Truly Help*. Chicago: Moody, 2020.

Hunt, June. *Counseling Through Your Bible Handbook: Providing Biblical Hope and Practical Help for Everyday Problems*. Eugene, OR: Harvest House Publishers, 2008.

Jenkins, Laura. *Thought Garden: Growing Healthy Thoughts with the Master Gardner.* [United States]: Self-Published by Laura Jenkins, 2021.

Keller, Timothy. *Walking with God through Pain and Suffering.* New York: Dutton, 2013.

Kellen, Kristin, and Julia Higgins. *The Whole Woman: Ministering to Her Heart, Soul, Mind, and Strength.* Nashville: B&H Publishing, 2021.

Lewis, C. S. *The Problem of Pain.* New York: MacMillan, 1962.

Ortlund, Dane C. *Gentle and Lowly: The Heart of Jesus for Sinners and Sufferers.* Wheaton, IL: Crossway, 2020.

Poarch, Brenda Barnes. *Side by Side: Learning to Share and Bear Life's Burdens.* Huntsville, AL: Publishing Designs, 2018.

Sande, Ken. *The Peacemaker: A Biblical Guide to Resolving Personal Conflicts.* 3rd edition. Grand Rapids: Baker, 2003.

Sumner, Sarah. *Angry Like Jesus: Using His Example to Spark Moral Courage.* Minneapolis: Fortress Press, 2015.

Townsend, John. *Boundaries with Teens: When to Say Yes, How to Say No.* Grand Rapids: Zondervan, 2006.

Tripp, Paul David. *War of Words: Getting to the Heart of Your Communication Struggles.* Phillipsburg, NJ: P&R Publishing Company, 2000.

———. *Instruments in the Redeemer's Hands: People in Need of Change Helping People in Need of Change.* Phillipsburg, NJ: P&R Publishing Company, 2002.

———. *Lost in the Middle: Midlife and the Grace of God.* Wapwallopen, PA: Shepherd Press, 2004.

Wilhelm, Jack P. and Bill Bagents. *Easing Life's Hurts.* 2nd ed. Florence, AL: Cypress Publications, 2020.

Acknowledgments

If you have ever embarked on a large project, you know that you are not able to do it by yourself. Writing a book is no exception. I would like to acknowledge some special individuals that God has providentially placed in my life, and for that, I am forever grateful.

I would not have the Bible and counseling knowledge I have today without Heritage Christian University. Everyone associated with HCU loves the Lord and strives to make a positive difference every day. I had phenomenal professors that made me think about Scripture in ways I had never before. They exposed me to a world of Theology, Biblical Studies, and academic resources that contributed to my learning. Thank you to Dr. Kirk Brothers, Dr. Jeremy Barrier, and Dr. Jeffrey Brothers for stretching my mind and making me a better Bible student.

Thank you to Dr. Michael Jackson, who is a friend who loves Disney as much as I do! Thank you for overseeing my Practicum defense and offering your input on how to expand this project. You are always encouraging me, and that is such a blessing!

Thank you to Dr. Bill Bagents, whom I am blessed to call a mentor and friend. Thank you for being a great encourager and wonderful professor. Thank you for sharing your wisdom of the Bible and counseling through your classes and answering my emails with any and every question I had. The support you have shown to me while writing this book was invaluable and will not be forgotten.

Thank you to Heritage Christian University Press for your dedication and publication of the book that I envisioned.

Thank you to Dr. Brad McKinnon for your patience and guidance as we worked together to create the book cover and made sure I was happy with it.

Thank you to the Elders at West Huntsville Church of Christ for giving me the opportunity to work with the counseling ministry in our congregation and for the support and encouragement you have shown to me. The insight I have gained from this experience has added to the richness of this book.

Thank you to Glenn Colley, Paul Owen, and Darren Crowden for your unwavering support and guidance you have provided me.

Thank you to Dr. Rosemary Snodgrass, Cindy Colley, Debbie Kea, and Cayron Mann for your encouragement and your example to me as sisters in Christ.

Thank you to Dana Glasscock for being a friend and true sister in Christ. Your encouragement and support will always be cherished.

Finally, to Michael, Adam, and Cynthia, you are my world, and I am thankful to God for you.

Also by Cypress Publications

The Christian Life: Chapters for Bible Teachers
by Ed Gallegher

Easing Life's Hurts
by Jack Wilhelm and Bill Bagents

Ecclesiastes: A Document Designed to Disturb
by Coy Roper

Equipping the Saints: A Practical Study of Ephesians 4:11–16
by Bill Bagents and Cory Collins

Jesus the Christ: Chapters for Bible Teachers
by Ed Gallagher

The Pre-Exilic Prophets: A Commentary and Reflection
by Blake Hayes

*Silly Songs, Surprising Stories, and Supreme Court Justices: The Wild
Fun-tier of Stone-Campbell Movement History* by John Young

*WHAM! Facing Life's Heavy Hits: Thirteen New Testament
Encounters* by Bill Bagents and Laura S. Bagents

*WHAM! Facing Life's Heavy Hits: Thirteen Old Testament
Encounters* by Bill Bagents and Laura S. Bagents

CYPRESS
PUBLICATIONS
An Imprint of Heritage Christian University Press

To see a full catalog of Heritage Christian University Press and
its imprint Cypress Publications, visit
www.hcu.edu/publications

www.ingramcontent.com/pod-product-compliance
Lightning Source LLC
Chambersburg PA
CBHW021108130626
46554CB00002B/588